DEADLY DISEASES AND EPIDEMICS

TETANUS

DEADLY DISEASES AND EPIDEMICS

Antibiotic-Resistant Bacteria

Anthrax

Avian Flu

Botulism

Campylobacteriosis

Cervical Cancer

Cholera

Dengue Fever and Other Hemorrhagic Viruses

Ebola

Encephalitis

Escherichia coli Infections

Gonorrhea

Hantavirus Pulmonary Syndrome

Heliobacter pylori

Hepatitis

Herpes

HIV/AIDS

Infectious Diseases of the Mouth

Infectious Fungi

Influenza

Legionnaires' Disease

Leprosy

Lung Cancer

Lyme Disease

Mad Cow Disease (Bovine Spongiform Encephalopathy)

Malaria

Meningitis

Mononucleosis

Pelvic Inflammatory Disease

Plague

Polio

Prostate Cancer

Rabies

Rocky Mountain Spotted Fever

Salmonella

SARS

Smallpox

Staphylococcus aureus Infections

Streptococcus (Group A)

Streptococcus (Group B)

Syphilis

Tetanus

Toxic Shock Syndrome

Trypanosomiasis

Tuberculosis

Tularemia

Typhoid Fever

West Nile Virus

DEADLY DISEASES AND EPIDEMICS

TETANUS

Patrick Guilfoile, Ph.D.

CONSULTING EDITOR
Hilary Babcock, M.D., M.P.H.,
Infectious Diseases Division,
Washington University School of Medicine,
Medical Director of Occupational Health (Infectious Diseases),
Barnes-Jewish Hospital and St. Louis Children's Hospital

FOREWORD BY
David Heymann
World Health Organization

CHELSEA HOUSE
PUBLISHERS
An imprint of Infobase Publishing

This book is dedicated to my wife, Audrey, and to my parents, Thomas and Jeannine Guilfoile, who have always been supportive of my writing.

Deadly Diseases and Epidemics: Tetanus

Copyright © 2008 by Infobase Publishing

Chelsea House
An imprint of Infobase Publishing
132 West 31st Street
New York, NY 10001

Library of Congress Cataloging-in-Publication Data
Guilfoile, Patrick.
    Tetanus / Patrick Guilfoile ; consulting editor, Hilary Babcock ; foreword by David Heymann.
        p. cm.—(Deadly diseases and epidemics)
    Includes bibliographical references and index.
    ISBN-13: 978-0-7910-9711-3
    ISBN-10: 0-7910-9711-0
    1. Tetanus—Popular works. I. Babcock, Hilary. II. Title.
    RC185.G85 2008
    616.9'318—dc22
                                    2007037928

Chelsea House books are available at special discounts when purchased in bulk quantities for businesses, associations, institutions, or sales promotions. Please call our Special Sales Department in New York at (212) 967-8800 or (800) 322-8755.

You can find Chelsea House on the World Wide Web at http://www.chelseahouse.com

Series design by Terry Mallon
Cover design by Takeshi Takahashi and Jooyoung An
Printed in the United States of America
Bang EJB 10 9 8 7 6 5 4 3 2 1
This book is printed on acid-free paper.

All links and Web addresses were checked and verified to be correct at the time of publication. Because of the dynamic nature of the Web, some addresses and links may have changed since publication and may no longer be valid.

Table of Contents

Foreword
David Heymann, World Health Organization   **6**

Acknowledgements   **8**

1. What Is Tetanus?   10

2. Tetanus in History   20

3. How Does *Clostridium tetani* Cause Disease?   38

4. How Is Tetanus Treated?   48

5. How Is Tetanus Prevented?   55

6. Continuing Concerns and Current Status of Tetanus   64

7. Future Prospects Regarding Tetanus   72

Endnotes   83

Glossary   89

Further Resources   93

Index   94

About the Author   100

About the Consulting Editor   100

Foreword

In the 1960s, many of the infectious diseases that had terrorized generations were tamed. After a century of advances, the leading killers of Americans both young and old were being prevented with new vaccines or cured with new medicines. The risk of death from pneumonia, tuberculosis (TB), meningitis, influenza, whooping cough, and diphtheria declined dramatically. New vaccines lifted the fear that summer would bring polio, and a global campaign was on the verge of eradicating smallpox worldwide. New pesticides like DDT cleared mosquitoes from homes and fields, thus reducing the incidence of malaria, which was present in the southern United States and which remains a leading killer of children worldwide. New technologies produced safe drinking water and removed the risk of cholera and other water-borne diseases. Science seemed unstoppable. Disease seemed destined to all but disappear.

But the euphoria of the 1960s has evaporated.

The microbes fought back. Those causing diseases like TB and malaria evolved resistance to cheap and effective drugs. The mosquito developed the ability to defuse pesticides. New diseases emerged, including AIDS, Legionnaires', and Lyme disease. And diseases which had not been seen in decades reemerged, as the hantavirus did in the Navajo Nation in 1993. Technology itself actually created new health risks. The global transportation network, for example, meant that diseases like West Nile virus could spread beyond isolated regions and quickly become global threats. Even modern public health protections sometimes failed, as they did in 1993 in Milwaukee, Wisconsin, resulting in 400,000 cases of the digestive system illness cryptosporidiosis. And, more recently, the threat from smallpox, a disease believed to be completely eradicated, has returned along with other potential bioterrorism weapons such as anthrax.

The lesson is that the fight against infectious diseases will never end.

In our constant struggle against disease, we as individuals have a weapon that does not require vaccines or drugs, and that is the warehouse of knowledge. We learn from the history of science that "modern" beliefs can be wrong. In this series of books, for example, you will learn that diseases like syphilis were once thought to be caused by eating potatoes. The invention of the microscope set science on the right path. There are more positive lessons from history. For example, smallpox was eliminated by vaccinating everyone who had come in contact with an infected person. This "ring" approach to smallpox control is still the preferred method for confronting an outbreak, should the disease be intentionally reintroduced.

At the same time, we are constantly adding new drugs, new vaccines, and new information to the warehouse. Recently, the entire human genome was decoded. So too was the genome of the parasite that causes malaria. Perhaps by looking at the microbe and the victim through the lens of genetics we will be able to discover new ways to fight malaria, which remains the leading killer of children in many countries.

Because of advances in our understanding of such diseases as AIDS, entire new classes of antiretroviral drugs have been developed. But resistance to all these drugs has already been detected, so we know that AIDS drug development must continue.

Education, experimentation, and the discoveries that grow out of them are the best tools to protect health. Opening this book may put you on the path of discovery. I hope so, because new vaccines, new antibiotics, new technologies, and, most importantly, new scientists are needed now more than ever if we are to remain on the winning side of this struggle against microbes.

David Heymann
Executive Director
Communicable Diseases Section
World Health Organization
Geneva, Switzerland

Acknowledgements

Thanks to Robyn Schulke and Pat Conely, Interlibrary loan staff at the Bemidji State University's A.C. Clark Library, for their outstanding assistance in securing a large number of old and obscure references. The state of Minnesota has an excellent interlibrary loan service (MnPALS) and the availability of that resource was essential for getting this book completed. I also thank Charles Fredrickson for translating several French journal articles and Gretchen Hemstock for translating several German journal articles. Finally, I wish to thank my son Forrest, who reviewed a draft of this book and offered constructive comments from the perspective of a high school student.

1
What Is Tetanus?

An elderly woman in England was recently brought into the emergency room of a hospital. Two days earlier, she had gotten a small scratch on her arm while gardening. She initially developed lockjaw, and recalling a previous bout with tetanus she had experienced almost 50 years earlier, she called the ambulance to take her to the hospital. In her case, the symptoms progressed to the appearance of a fixed smile (called **risus sardonicus***) and painful muscle spasms, the classical presentation of tetanus. Her treatment required the use of a ventilator for almost three weeks and numerous medications, but she survived. She had been given one tetanus vaccination in middle age, but that wasn't sufficient to protect her for this long. Following her treatment, she was given two additional tetanus vaccinations, which would be expected to protect her from the disease for at least another 10 years.*[1]

Tetanus is a frequently fatal disease caused by the bacterium *Clostridium tetani*. The disease is characterized by intense, painful muscle contractions, sometimes strong enough to break even the strongest bones in the body. Reflecting the symptoms of the disease, the word *tetanus* is derived from the Greek term *tetanos*, meaning "to contract."

Historically, tetanus had a high mortality rate. With the limited medical treatment available in the 1940s in the United States, for example, the death rate for tetanus was estimated to be over 90 percent.[2] Even with intensive medical treatment, the death rate is still 5 to 10 percent.

One reason that tetanus continues to be a problem is that *C. tetani* is widely distributed in the environment. In a study conducted by researchers at the Harvard School of Public Health in the 1960s, **toxin**-producing strains of *C. tetani* were found in three of 18 (or 17 percent) environmental samples collected in Boston.[3] A similar report by a researcher at

Johns Hopkins University from 1937 described the analysis of street dust from Baltimore, Maryland. In this case, nine of 63 (or 14 percent) samples contained toxin-producing *C. tetani*, suggesting that this **pathogen** (disease-causing microbe) was widely distributed in another urban environment.[4] *C. tetani* has been found in the intestines and fecal material of humans and other animals, so it is thought to be common in the soil in rural areas as well. A study, from 1922, by Tenbroeck and Bauer of the Peking Union Medical College, found that about one-third of 78 human stool samples examined contained *C. tetani*.[5] However, a more recent survey found no evidence of *C. tetani* in fecal samples from 100 humans in Massachusetts,[3] suggesting that the likelihood of ingesting *C. tetani* varies in different regions.

Another reason that tetanus is still a problem is that *C. tetani* produces **spores**, which allow this organism to

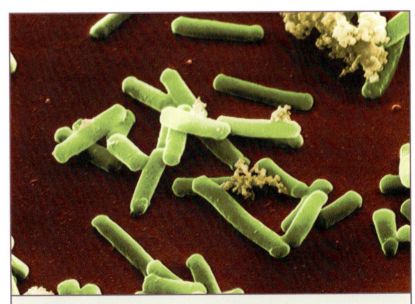

Figure 1.1   Photograph of *C. Tetani* taken through a light microscope. (Eye of Science/Photo Researchers, Inc.)

survive for decades in an inert state. Spores are an extremely resistant form of the microbe that protects the bacterium from many otherwise potent strategies for destroying pathogens. Spores of C. tetani can survive being heated in a water bath at 80°C (176°F) for at least an hour, being exposed to UV light for long periods, and contacting a variety of disinfectants and cleaning agents. For example, spores of the genus Clostridium can be isolated from other bacteria by treatment with ethyl alcohol. After one hour of treatment with ethyl alcohol, other bacteria are killed, but the C. tetani spores remain viable.[6] There has even been a report of spores (from a different species) surviving millions of years in the gut of a bee that was preserved in amber.[7] Therefore, once spores are present in an area, in terms of human lifetimes, they are essentially eternal.

CHARACTERISTICS OF TETANUS

C. tetani typically enters the body through a wound. The spores will germinate and grow only if the wound is deprived of oxygen. This is why stepping on a nail is a common way for a person to acquire tetanus. (About 12 percent of tetanus infections in the United States from 1998–2000 were the result of a person stepping on a nail.) A deep wound in the foot will often be poorly supplied with oxygen, allowing C. tetani to grow. During growth, the bacteria start producing the tetanus toxin, **tetanospasmin**. On average it is about a week between the time a person is infected with the bacterium and the time symptoms appear. However, a substantial number of tetanus patients had no known injury prior to the development of tetanus.

In some of these cases, tetanus spores may have been introduced into a wound weeks to years earlier. The wound may have healed up with the spores inside, but the site had too high an oxygen content to allow cells to grow. At some point, that site may eventually have become deprived of oxygen, allowing the spores to germinate, producing actively growing C. tetani cells that produce the tetanus toxin, tetanospasmin.

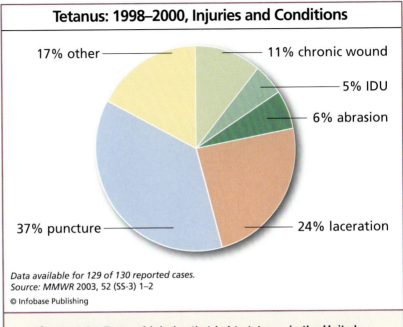

Tetanus: 1998–2000, Injuries and Conditions

17% other

11% chronic wound

5% IDU

6% abrasion

37% puncture

24% laceration

Data available for 129 of 130 reported cases.
Source: MMWR 2003, 52 (SS-3) 1–2
© Infobase Publishing

Figure 1.2 Types of injuries that led to tetanus in the United States, 1998–2000. Data available for 129 of 130 reported cases. (IDU = injecting drug use)

Tetanospasmin is transported in the tissues until it reaches a **motor neuron** (a nerve that controls a muscle). The toxin enters the nerve and then is transported back up the nerve to the spinal cord. Once in the spinal cord, tetanus toxin exits the motor neuron and enters an **inhibitory neuron** (a neuron in the spinal cord that normally prevents muscle contraction). Once inside the inhibitory neuron, tetanus toxin prevents the release of **neurotransmitters** (chemicals released by one nerve cell that control the activities of another nerve cell); the consequence is that there is no inhibition of muscle contraction. This ultimately leads to violent contractions of all the major muscle groups.

The symptoms of tetanus typically start four to 14 days following infection, although in recent cases in the United

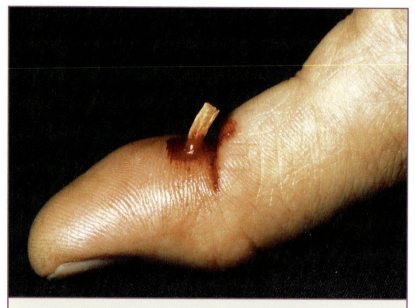

Figure 1.3 Close-up of a splinter of wood in the finger of a 40-year-old woman. Even minor injuries such as this may lead to tetanus. (Dr. P. Marazz/Photo Researchers, Inc.)

States 15 percent had a shorter incubation period than four days, and 12 percent had an incubation period longer than 14 days.[8] Typically (in about 75 percent of the cases), individuals developing tetanus initially have difficulty moving their jaw ("lockjaw" or *trismus*) and frequently have a fixed smile called *risus sardonicus*. This is because the distance between the peripheral nerves and the spinal cord is the shortest for the muscles that control the jaw and for other facial muscles. Once the toxin enters one of those nerves it reaches the spinal cord quickly. If left untreated more muscles become affected as more toxin reaches the spinal cord, and the infected person develops widespread muscle spasms. These spasms are extremely painful and become more and more constant. An affected person frequently arches his or her back during muscle spasms in a distinctive posture called **opisthotonos**. The smallest stimulus (a faint noise, turning on a light) can trigger the muscle spasms. At this point, which may occur within a few days of the initial symptom of lockjaw, the nerves that regulate

WHY IS THIS TOXIN SO POTENT?

The answer to this question is not completely known, but a reasonable hypothesis can be made. It is often thought that well-adapted pathogens rarely kill their hosts. However, *C. tetani* is an obligate anaerobe, meaning that it will grow only in environments lacking oxygen. A dead animal quickly becomes anaerobic, because no new oxygen is brought into its body (since the animal can no longer breathe), and existing bacteria use up the remaining oxygen. So, by killing its host, *C. tetani* creates a large, favorable environment for its reproduction. Since *C. tetani* produces environmentally resistant spores, once the bacteria are released from the dead body, they can survive in the soil for many, many years. Therefore, killing its host may be a useful mechanism for ensuring that *C. tetani* can grow and reproduce.

Why is the toxin so potent? Bacteria and animals are involved in a continuing struggle to cause (in the case of bacteria) and control (in the case of animals) infection. This struggle takes place between the pathogen and the immune system. One key aspect of the immune system is that, following an illness, a second exposure to a pathogen will typically result in such a strong response that the pathogen is eliminated, often before any symptoms of a disease surface. *C. tetani* circumvents this important protection by producing a toxin so potent that it is effective in amounts too small to activate the immune system. Therefore, if an animal is infected with the bacteria and somehow manages to survive, on second exposure, the animal will be as susceptible to the toxin as it was the first time, and will still be likely to die and create a favorable environment for growth of *C. tetani*.

respiration may stop functioning and a person can die from the inability to breathe. In addition, nervous system control of the heart can be affected, leading to erratic heartbeat that can cause the heart to malfunction.

TETANUS DISEASE PRESENTATIONS

Tetanus occurs in one of four forms, which are classified based on toxin distribution in the body, symptoms of the disease, and the age of the victims.

Generalized tetanus is the most common form of tetanus in developed countries. In this manifestation of tetanus, the toxin affects the nerves throughout the body, resulting in spasms in many of the major muscle groups. About 80 percent of tetanus cases in the United States fall into this category.

Localized tetanus, as the name suggests, leads to stiffness and spasm in the area adjacent to a wound containing *C. tetani*. In some cases, this can lead to generalized tetanus, but normally the symptoms are much milder, and historically, localized tetanus has had a relatively low fatality rate.

Cephalic tetanus typically occurs when *C. tetani* grows in a head wound or gets into the ear canal and starts a middle ear infection. The primary symptom is facial paralysis, caused by action of the toxin on the cranial nerves. In some cases, if left untreated, this can also progress to generalized tetanus.

Neonatal tetanus occurs when an infant is infected with *C. tetani*, frequently through the umbilical cord. It occurs when the mother hasn't been **immunized** against tetanus; if the mother has been immunized, **antibodies** pass from the mother to the infant, offering protection against the disease for the first months of life. (Antibodies are proteins produced by a type of white blood cell called a B-cell that can help prevent infection with microbes, such as those that cause tetanus.) Although rare in developed countries, neonatal tetanus causes the greatest number of human tetanus deaths worldwide.

DISORDERS THAT MIGHT INITIALLY BE CONFUSED WITH TETANUS

Tetanus is diagnosed based on the distinctive symptoms of the disease. Frequently no bacteria can be isolated from a wound and toxin normally cannot be detected in the blood, particularly early in the course of infection, so laboratory tests are often not very revealing. Even though the severe muscle spasms in later stages of the disease are unmistakable, the early symptoms can be confused with other maladies. These other afflictions include

- strychnine poisoning (which can be identified with a blood test)

- dislocations of the mandible (which would produce lock-jaw, but would, unlike tetanus, cause a great deal of pain in the jaw joint)

- black widow spider bites (which can cause generalized muscle cramps—a history of a spider bite is important in differentiating this illness from tetanus)

- certain types of stroke (which may lead to seizures that mimic tetanus muscle contractions)

- infections of the central nervous system (which can cause neck stiffness, even leading to an arching of the neck, reminiscent of tetanus)

- rabies (whose symptoms can include difficulty swallowing, but there is normally history of an animal bite)

- tooth abscesses (which can lead to difficulty in opening the mouth)

- and some other conditions

Time is of the essence in starting treatment for tetanus, so it is important that a physician quickly differentiate between tetanus and other conditions that show some of the same or similar symptoms.

TETANUS AND THE INFECTION OF OTHER HOSTS

Tetanus infection causes similar disease in a wide variety of other vertebrate animals. Frogs are susceptible, and tetanus toxin causes spastic muscle paralysis in all, or almost all, mammals. Most susceptible are horses, guinea pigs, monkeys, sheep, mice, and goats. Other mammals and birds, including cats, dogs, pigeons, and geese, can also be infected with *C. tetani*, but they appear to require a larger dose of toxin for symptoms to develop.

Tetanus toxin has similar effects on the nerve cells of a variety of invertebrates including crayfish, squid, leeches, and fruit flies. The difference in susceptibility of different animals to tetanus toxin probably reflects slight differences in the type of molecules present on the surface of their nerve cells. It seems likely that the molecules on the most sensitive animals most readily facilitate the entry of the toxin into the nerves.

The limited amount of data available suggests that humans are very susceptible to tetanus toxin. In one case, for example, children were injected with diphtheria antitoxin (antiserum) from a horse, in order to treat their diphtheria infection. Unfortunately, the horse that provided the serum was infected with *C. tetani*, and developed symptoms of tetanus shortly after the serum was collected. Sadly, 13 children died from tetanus as a result of receiving the tainted serum. When this horse serum was tested, 0.1 cubic centimeter was sufficient to cause fatal tetanus in a guinea pig. Based on the amount of horse serum (diphtheria antitoxin) the children had received, the authors determined that humans are only slightly less susceptible to tetanus toxin, pound for pound, compared to guinea pigs.[9]

This incident was the worst case of tetanus toxin contamination of drugs in the United States, but there have been other incidents. For example, there were nine deaths from tetanus in children in Camden, New Jersey, following vaccination. These incidents and others led the U.S. Congress to pass the Biologics Control Act of 1902. This act required inspections and licensing of companies that manufactured vaccines, antitoxins, and related therapeutics. These drugs had to be appropriately labeled, and a government agency was charged with testing these biologics for purity and potency. In 1972, these functions became part of the work of the U.S. Food and Drug Administration.[10]

2

Tetanus in History

"The Master of a large ship mashed the index finger of his right hand with the anchor. Seven days later a somewhat foul discharge appeared; then trouble with his tongue—he complained he could not speak properly. The presence of tetanus was diagnosed, his jaws became pressed together, his teeth were locked, then symptoms appeared in his neck; on the third day opisthotonos appeared with sweating. Six days after the diagnosis was made he died."

—Hippocrates, 425 B.C.[11]

Reports of tetanus date back to the earliest historical records. For example, the Edwin Smith Surgical Papyrus, from the seventeenth century B.C., has descriptions of patients with wounds who have symptoms of neck stiffness and tight ligaments, likely the first known description of tetanus. In that era when a patient was likely to have tetanus the physician was supposed to state to him, "I will not contend," meaning the doctors then had no means of treating it.[12]

Hippocrates provided another detailed descriptions of the symptoms of tetanus in his work "Epidemics" around 425 B.C.

> . . . Tychon the soldier had received an arrow in his back. The wound seemed quite minor, since the missile entered at a sharp angle [and was] easily [removed]. . . . [That night] as dusk settled, the soldiers posted their pickets. The camp began to hear low moans from where Tychon had built his cooking fire; moans soon became grunts and what sounded like someone gnashing his teeth in a fury of rage. . . . Tychon . . . was alone, moaning in the most curious posture: he was arched back in opisthotonos and his jaws seemed locked together

against his will.... A friend forced some wine between his teeth, but Tychon could not swallow, and the liquid was expelled in spurts from his nostrils.... [In the morning, two days later] as a cock crowed his welcome to the first rays of the dawn, Tychon died.[13]

Aretaeus, the Cappadocian, a first century Greek physician wrote perhaps one of the most compelling descriptions of tetanus.

An inhuman calamity! An unseemly sight! A spectacle even painful to the beholder! An incurable malady! ... the physician, though present and looking on, [cannot] furnish any assistance.... Should he try to straighten the patient's body, he would have to dissect or break it. This is the great misfortune of the physician.[14]

HISTORICAL FIGURES OR CELEBRITIES WHO DIED OF TETANUS

Not even the rich, famous, or powerful have been immune to tetanus throughout history.

King Rajasinghe (1592) of the Sithawatke Kingdom, Sri Lanka (Ceylon): A recent report raised the question of whether his tetanus was deliberately induced. His physician, under the influence of a rival prince, covered the king's foot wound with plant material mixed with cow and horse dung, material likely to contain tetanus spores and cause tetanus.[15] A description of his symptoms was consistent with tetanus, including the reports that he had a smile on his face while he was dying (likely the fixed smile known as *risus sardonicus*, which is a common symptom of tetanus).

Johann Tserclaes (1632): A general for the Holy Roman Empire; died from tetanus after being wounded by a cannon ball during battle.

George Montagu (1815): An important early naturalist, particularly in the study of birds in England; contracted tetanus when he stepped on a nail.

John Thoreau I (1842): Brother of Henry David Thoreau. He got a small cut on his thumb, and died three days after he showed symptoms of the disease. In an account of his death, the impression was that his passing was somewhat peaceful and serene, a contrast with what would be expected for someone dying from tetanus.[16]

George Crockett Strong (1863): Union brigadier general in the American Civil War; contracted tetanus from wounds sustained in a Civil War battle in South Carolina.

John A. Roebling (1869): Architect who designed the Brooklyn Bridge; contracted tetanus following amputation of his toes. He was trying to determine the location of a tower for the bridge when his foot was injured by a ferry boat, which crashed into the wharf where he was standing.

Joe Powell (1896): English soccer player; he broke his arm during a game and developed tetanus as a result of the injury.

Fred Thomson (1928): Silent film actor; contracted tetanus after stepping on a nail while working in his horse stable.

THE IDENTIFICATION OF *CLOSTRIDIUM TETANI*

Prior to the late 1800s microbes were not known to cause disease. Other factors like bad air, an imbalance of fluids in the body, or other environmental causes were thought to be the basis of most illnesses. Eventually, though, it became clear that tetanus and other diseases were caused by microbes.

The nature of tetanus as an infectious disease was discovered in 1884 by several researchers. Antonio Carle and Giorgio Rattone[18] first reported evidence that tetanus was an infectious disease in that year. They removed a pus-filled wound from the neck of a patient who had just died of tetanus and injected this material into 12 rabbits. Of the 12 animals, 11 died of tetanus. They removed the nerves from four of the rabbits afflicted with tetanus and injected that material into two rabbits, both of which quickly succumbed to tetanus. Carle and Rattone thought that the microbe causing the disease was present in the nerves. Their hypothesis was based on the work of Louis

TETANUS AND THE DEPOPULATION OF ST. KILDA

An isolated island off the cost of Scotland, St. Kilda had a major outbreak of neonatal tetanus during the 1800s. Between 1855 and 1876, 41 infants (out of 56 total births) died of the "sickness of eight days," which was neonatal tetanus. At the time, the traditional practice among midwives in Scotland was to cover the umbilical cord with salt butter or oil. Butter was scarce on the island, so in its place midwives used oil from a local bird called a fulmar. This oil was stored in a bag made of a dried goose stomach, and likely was heavily contaminated with tetanus spores. An enlightened minister eventually convinced the midwives to change their practices, and by the 1890s neonatal tetanus was no longer a problem on the island. However, the island was abandoned by the last 36 inhabitants in 1930, and it has been speculated that this happened, in part, because of the high infant death rate during the 1800s.[17]

Pasteur on the rabies virus. Although the rabies virus invades the nerve cells, it is now known that the tetanus bacterium remains in the wound, and only the toxin travels to the nerves. Because they continued to look for *C. tetani* in the nerves, they were never able to isolate the organism that causes tetanus and do additional research.

Also in 1884, Arthur Nicolaier[19] reported that when he injected soil particles into dogs, mice, rabbits, and guinea pigs, in some cases the animals died of tetanus. Furthermore, when he microscopically examined the bacterial population at the site of the injection he found a mixed group of microbes, including thin, rod-shaped organisms that he felt were responsible for the disease. He also grew the organisms in sheep blood serum in the laboratory. Although he didn't get the tetanus bacterium to grow apart from other bacteria, Nicolaier was able to induce tetanus in experimental animals by injecting material taken from the bottom of the tubes of sheep blood serum. These findings suggested that a specific bacterium caused tetanus, and that the organism that caused tetanus lived in the soil. Nicolaier also indicated that the bacteria stayed at the site of initial infection, but produced a toxin similar to the poison **strychnine**, which caused the symptoms of tetanus. He found that soil from many different environments harbored the bacteria that cause tetanus, suggesting that these microbes were widely distributed in nature.

The isolation of *C. tetani*, and the clear association of this organism with tetanus, was made in 1889 by Shibasburo Kitasato.[20] At the time Kitasato worked in the lab of Dr. Robert Koch, who was one of the world's leading microbiologists. Koch had recently identified the bacterium responsible for causing anthrax, so his laboratory was filled with researchers trying to discover the causative agents of other important human diseases.

The first step in Kitasato's work was to isolate the tetanus bacterium in pure culture. This meant that the bacterium had to be separated from all the other bacterial species that might be present in a sample. This was a potentially challenging task.

Kitasato isolated 16 different types of bacteria—including, presumably, the bacterium that causes tetanus—from pus taken from a soldier who had recently died of this disease. Initially he wasn't able to get the tetanus bacterium to grow separately from the other bacteria.

Fortunately, Kitasato discovered that *C. tetani* spores were much more heat resistant than most other bacteria present in wounds or other environments. This was a great aid in isolating the tetanus bacterium in pure culture. He could heat a sample containing tetanus spores to 80°C for about an hour, killing other contaminating bacteria without harming the *C. tetani* spores.

But he also had to determine what conditions were required for growth of the *C. tetani* in the absence of other bacteria. One

Figure 2.1 Shibasburo Kitasato first isolated *C. tetani.* (National Library of Medicine)

of his critical observations was that *C. tetani* could grow only in the absence of oxygen; he knew this because it only formed colonies in the lower portions of agar medium that were lacking this element. This meant that special conditions and procedures would be required to grow the organism in the laboratory—specifically, the use of a hydrogen atmosphere above the cultures to exclude oxygen. By heating samples containing *C. tetani* to kill contaminating bacteria and anaerobic incubation, he was able to grow, in pure culture, the organism he thought caused tetanus.

The next step was testing animals to verify that these microbes did, indeed, cause tetanus. He demonstrated that infection of mice with pure cultures of this bacterium led to tetanus, that the microbes could be isolated from the infected mice, and that pure cultures of this bacterium could cause the same disease in a new batch of mice. Kitasato also injected mice with various soil samples, observed that the mice developed tetanus, and then isolated the tetanus bacteria from the dead mice. He noted that these bacteria were the same as the bacteria that he had previously isolated in pure culture.

Kitasato was able to optimize the conditions for growing the bacteria, determining that they grow best at 36°C to 38°C, in slightly alkaline conditions, with proteins as a major nutrient source. This would become critical in later work, because the bacteria had to be grown in large quantities in order to produce a drug to treat tetanus and, ultimately, a vaccine to prevent it. He also confirmed Nicolaier's observation that the bacteria were present only at the site where they were injected into the body, and that they did not spread to other organs and tissues, suggesting that the bacteria produced a toxin that travels through the body.

Further work by Sanchez-Toledo and Veillon demonstrated that the bacterium was a regular cell in the intestines of animals, but a resistant spore in the soil. Knud Faber, a Danish scientist, first reported isolating tetanus toxin, separate from *C. tetani*, in 1890. He reported that animals injected with culture fluid containing the toxin, but filtered to remove bacteria, developed disease symptoms identical to those caused by infection with *C. tetani*.[21]

THE DISCOVERY OF TETANUS ANTITOXIN (TETANUS IMMUNOGLOBULIN)

The first report of the potential for antitoxin to prevent death due to tetanus was published in 1890 by Emil Behring and Kitasato.[22] Initially they immunized rabbits against tetanus, presumably by injecting the rabbits with small doses of

tetanus bacteria that weren't lethal. Then they likely gradually increased the dose until they could inject 20 times the
amount of bacteria that would normally be deadly and the
rabbits would remain healthy. Next they took blood from the
immunized rabbits and injected either whole blood, or just
the serum (the liquid left after the blood has coagulated), into
mice. A short time later they injected mice with either *C. tetani* or tetanus toxin. The mice that had received the injection
of blood or serum survived, whereas control mice that did
not receive blood or serum died. This indicated that something in the blood could inactivate the toxin. That substance
in blood is now known to be antibodies. Blood or blood
products containing antibodies with the ability to neutralize
tetanus toxin is called **tetanus immunoglobulin**.

Figure 2.2   Emil von Behring (on the right), pictured here with a
lab assistant, won the 1901 Nobel Prize for his work with tetanus
and diphtheria immunizations.   (Bettmann/Corbis)

Further work on the development of antibodies as a therapy for tetanus was reported in 1895 by Edmond Nocard.[23] He produced large amounts of tetanus immunoglobulin, which was made available to veterinarians for treating animals before or immediately after surgery, or for treating animals that had injuries that may have become infected with *C. tetani*. Veterinarians treated 375 animals with tetanus immunoglobulin, and none of them developed tetanus. On the other hand, some untreated animals in the same areas, with similar surgeries or similar wounds, did develop tetanus. Although this didn't definitively establish that tetanus immunoglobulin protected the animals, it did provide evidence that supported the benefits of using this treatment. Other researchers extended these findings to humans—and in some cases extended them too far. Based on the understanding that tetanus had its effects on the central nervous system, and based on some experiments in guinea pigs, a few physicians felt that direct injection of tetanus immunoglobulin into the brain was more likely to cure patients than a typical injection under the skin. This technique was first reported by Chauffard and Quenu in France in 1898. It involved removing small pieces of bone from two sites on the skull and then injecting up to 2 cc of tetanus immunoglobulin directly into the brain 5 cm to 6 cm deep. Their first patient survived, but other patients died following this treatment, in some cases as the result of brain infections. However, this didn't dampen the enthusiasm for the therapy and it became used in many countries in Europe. By 1903, an analysis of the technique by Chipault showed this method worked no better than injecting tetanus immunoglobulin under the skin, and brain injections were abandoned.[24]

Collectively, these discoveries led to the development of an industry for the production of what are now known as **immunoglobulins** (antibodies). The work of Paul Ehrlich[25] was also critical for the further development of antibody therapy. He developed methods for standardizing antibody doses, which made the results of treatment more consistent and predictable from patient to patient.

Ultimately, these immunoglobulin treatments were widely used for several diseases, including tetanus and diphtheria. Horses were initially used for producing tetanus immuno-globulin. They were injected with increasing doses of tetanus toxin until they produced large amounts of antibodies. Blood was then taken from the horses and used to treat patients. In the United States human immunoglobulin has been used for treating tetanus since 1960, because of the potential for an allergic reaction to components of horse blood. This product comes from the blood of human donors who have been vac-cinated against tetanus.

TETANUS TOXOID VACCINE

A number of attempts were made, starting in the early 1900s, to develop an effective tetanus vaccine. One strategy involved injecting a mixture of active tetanus toxin and tetanus immu-noglobulin. But it was difficult to ensure that the tetanus toxin and antibody were present in the proper proportions, and that the antibody would continue to bind the toxin. This was a con-cern because if free toxin was present, the vaccine itself could cause tetanus.

Subsequent work in developing a vaccine against tetanus involved treating the tetanus toxin with chemicals to perma-nently inactivate the toxin. In a 1909 paper, German researcher Ernst Lowenstein described numerous chemical treatments that had been used in an attempt to detoxify tetanus toxin while preserving its ability to stimulate an immune response. A wide range of disinfectants (including formaldehyde), met-als, acid, bases, and physical factors (such as heat and light) were tested. Most of these treatments either had no effect on the toxin, or they degraded the toxin to such an extent that it no longer retained the ability to produce an immune response following vaccination. Ultimately Lowenstein's use of light to inactivate the toxin emerged as one of the most promising approaches, although further testing showed the importance of exposing the tetanus toxin to both formaldehyde and sunlight. He found that this dual treatment substantially decreased the toxicity of the tetanus toxin.[26]

One of the first attempts to vaccinate humans against tetanus was described in a 1915 paper by the German scientist Michael Eisler.[27] His experiments initially involved vaccinating guinea pigs and rabbits with tetanus toxin that had been treated with formaldehyde. Eventually he extended his work to include vaccinations of horses and two dozen humans. Although these treatments were apparently quite safe, the immune responses were not very vigorous. For example, the horses described in his paper had to be vaccinated with almost 2.5 liters of the treated tetanus toxin before they produced a large amount of antibody. In the human trials, patients received between 4 cc and 10 cc of the formaldehyde-treated tetanus toxin. However, subsequent tests indicated that these individuals did not develop much of an immune response to the toxin. Based on experiments in guinea pigs, the authors estimated that a total of 100 cc of the formaldehyde-treated tetanus toxin would have to be injected into a person to produce a substantial immune response. Considering that a typical vaccination today may contain 1 cc to 3 cc of liquid, this vaccine preparation was not very effective.

Another early attempt to vaccinate humans against tetanus was reported in 1917 by the French researchers Vallee and Bazy.[28] World War I was still raging at the time of their experiments, and the many seriously wounded soldiers provided an impetus to develop new methods to prevent tetanus. Their work involved treating a solution of tetanus toxin with a mixture of iodine and potassium iodide. They tested this preparation on seven soldiers of African ancestry who had received serious wounds at a section of the front known to contain *C. tetani* in the soil. Many of these soldiers suffered from additional complications like frostbite or broken limbs, which the researchers felt placed them at high risk for contracting tetanus. They reported that their vaccine caused no harm to the patients, and none of them developed tetanus a month after the third vaccination. Vallee and Bazy also tested this toxin preparation on rabbits, and found that those receiving a dose equivalent to that given to their human patients resisted a dose of toxin that was capable of killing 400 unvaccinated guinea pigs. Further testing, though, apparently established that this vaccine was not very safe or stable, and it was abandoned.

In 1911 Gaston Ramon started work at the Pasteur Institute in Paris, France. His previous training was in veterinary science, which prepared him well for his duties at the Institute. Initially his work involved producing large amounts of tetanus and diphtheria immunoglobulins (antibodies or antitoxins) from horses. To produce the immunoglobulins, he injected the animals with slowly increasing doses of active tetanus toxin until, eventually, the animals became immune, and they produced large amounts of antibodies to the toxin. Blood was then taken from the horses and allowed to clot. The liquid remaining after clotting was spun in a **centrifuge** (a machine that spins samples at a high speed, causing cells or small particles to form a pellet in the bottom of a tube) to remove blood cells that didn't get trapped in the clot. The liquid was then removed from the tube, and this liquid contained anti-tetanus

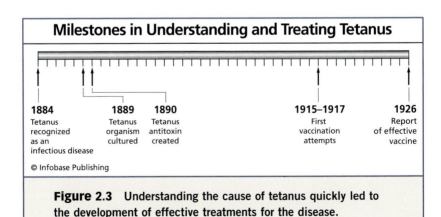

Milestones in Understanding and Treating Tetanus

1884	1889	1890	1915–1917	1926
Tetanus recognized as an infectious disease	Tetanus organism cultured	Tetanus antitoxin created	First vaccination attempts	Report of effective vaccine

© Infobase Publishing

Figure 2.3 Understanding the cause of tetanus quickly led to the development of effective treatments for the disease.

immunoglobulins. These immunoglobulins were then used to treat patients suffering from tetanus.

One of the technical problems Ramon encountered in this work was that the preparations of tetanus toxin would sometimes become contaminated with bacteria, which made them unusable. While in veterinary school Ramon worked with a faculty member, A. Monvoisin, who told him that milk could be preserved by adding a thimbleful (2 ml to 4 ml) of **formalin** (37 percent formaldehyde in water) per liter. (Since formaldehyde itself is toxic, this is certainly not currently a recommended preservative for any food.) Ramon tried using formaldehyde to inhibit the growth of contaminating bacteria in his toxin preparations. He found that treating tetanus toxin with this chemical preserved the toxin and rendered it inactive, yet left it capable of generating an immune response. These were the exact properties needed for an effective vaccine.

A problem with the previous work of Eisler, described above, was that he didn't have a way of testing the potency of his formaldehyde-treated vaccine prior to injecting it in animals. (In part, that could help explain the requirement for large doses of Eisler's vaccine.) Ramon encountered the same problem in testing his vaccine preparation (now called tetanus toxoid). The existing test for potency involved determining how much tetanus toxin was required to kill an animal. Since the formaldehyde had inactivated the toxin, he had to develop an alternative test to quantitate the amount of tetanus toxoid in a preparation. By 1922 Ramon had developed a system involving the use of antibodies. If the amount of toxoid equaled the amount of antibody in a test tube, a strong precipitate would be formed; if the amounts of toxin and antibody were not equal, the precipitate wouldn't be as pronounced. By varying the amount of antibody in different tubes, he could determine the exact amount of toxoid based on the amount of antibody that produced the strongest precipitate. Therefore, unlike Eisler, Ramon could precisely measure the amount of toxoid in his vaccine before he tested it in animals.

Ramon's student, Descombey, described the tetanus toxoid vaccine in detail in a 1924 paper.[29] The vaccine preparation (made by Lowenstein) was formulated by exposing the tetanus toxin to formaldehyde and heat. This vaccine was tested in guinea pigs and found to be both innocuous and highly effective. Within two to three months following vaccination, the animals would not suffer any ill effects after being injected with a dose of tetanus toxin sufficient to kill several thousand unvaccinated guinea pigs. Descombey wrote in the paper that this vaccine might prove useful for preventing tetanus in domestic animals.

Further tests of that conjecture were made in 1925 by Ramon and Descombey,[30] who tested tetanus toxoid vaccination in horses. One of the innovations they tried in these experiments was the use of an **adjuvant**, a chemical that, when added to a vaccine, increases its ability to cause the production of antibodies. They used finely ground tapioca (the same ingredient sometimes used to make pudding) as an adjuvant in some of the vaccine preparations. They found that following multiple vaccinations, horses that were injected with tetanus toxoid and tapioca could survive a dose of active tetanus toxin that would normally kill 10,000 horses. This was a great improvement over the same tetanus toxoid without the tapioca adjuvant, which would provide protection only against a much weaker dose of toxin—one that could kill 200 unvaccinated horses.

In 1926 Ramon and Zoller[31] described the use of formaldehyde-inactivated tetanus toxoid as a vaccine for humans. Essentially, nearly the same formulation is used today. Initially, one of their colleagues, Lafaille, tested the vaccine preparation on himself. Noting no ill effects on Lafaille, Ramon and Zoller then vaccinated 100 people with the tetanus toxoid. No harmful effects were noted in the people who were vaccinated. They found that a single dose of the vaccine did not result in the production of much antibody. This was based on the observation that 1 cc of blood serum drawn from test subjects did not contain enough antibody to neutralize the small amount of toxin required to kill a single guinea pig. However, those subjects who received two vaccinations had sufficient antibody in 1 cc of blood serum to neutralize toxin doses that would kill one to 10 guinea pigs (this variation illustrates the variation in the amount of antibody produced by different individuals). Those subjects who received a third dose of the vaccine had sufficient antibody in 1 cc of blood serum to neutralize an amount of tetanus toxin that would kill 1,000 to 3,000 guinea pigs. This was a much higher level of antibody production than Eisler had previously observed with his vaccine experiments. This information helped establish that multiple vaccinations are needed for people to be protected against tetanus. In addition Ramon and Zoller showed that this vaccine could be mixed with another vaccine to confer resistance to multiple pathogens with a single injection. This formed the basis for the modern DPT shot, which protects against diphtheria, pertussis, and tetanus, diseases caused by three different species of bacteria.

Most historians now attribute the development of the tetanus vaccine primarily to Ramon, since he perfected techniques for making and assaying a high potency preparation of tetanus toxoid. However, as noted above, like almost every scientific advance, many people contributed to the development of this important medical intervention.

When this tetanus toxoid vaccine first became available, there was some skepticism as to its value. For example, in 1937 Dr. Herman Gold wrote:

> In spite of the claims made by a number of biological houses sponsoring and marketing tetanus toxoid, the story of active immunization against tetanus is not completely known. Since it is still in the experimental stage, we ought to be cautious in its use; otherwise, we may run into cases of lockjaw in persons thought to be actively immunized. I feel that it will be useful in certain types

Figure 2.4 Gaston Ramon is credited with the discovery of the tetanus vaccine. (National Library of Medicine)

of medical practice, but I fear that it will not, from my present experience, be suitable for the general use which is being advocated for it at the present time.[32]

Despite pockets of skepticism, the vaccine became widely used in the United States in the 1940s. It was used by U.S. soldiers during World War II, and as a consequence, there

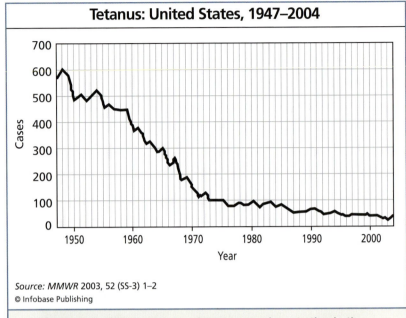

Figure 2.5   Widespread use of tetanus vaccine, starting in the 1940s, helped reduce tetanus cases in subsequent decades.

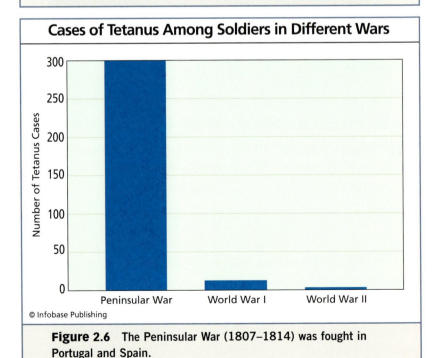

Figure 2.6   The Peninsular War (1807–1814) was fought in Portugal and Spain.

were only 12 tetanus cases among the 2.7 million soldiers with wounds treated at army hospitals during the war (a rate of 0.00044 percent). Of these tetanus cases, six were soldiers who had never been vaccinated, and an additional two of the 12 had not received a complete series of tetanus shots. In contrast, during World War I, before a vaccine was available, there were 70 cases and the rate of tetanus infection was about 30 times higher (0.013 percent of wounds led to tetanus). However, during World War I, **antitoxin** (tetanus immunoglobulin) was available and this reduced the incidence of tetanus. By contrast, the rate of tetanus among British soldiers in Spain during the Peninsular War in 1808–1814, before the availability of tetanus immunoglobulin, was 0.125 percent, about 10-fold higher than the rate during World War I, and about 250-fold higher, compared to the rate during World War II.[33] [34]

3

How Does *Clostridium tetani* Cause Disease?

Imagine a tiny tetanus spore, lying seemingly lifeless in a patch of soil for decades. The winds, rains, and snows each year have no effect on this forlorn spore. Then, as if by a miracle, a woodsman trips and gashes his shin with his axe as he falls. The wound is relatively minor, but as he gets up, the bit of dirt that contains the spore gets ground into the cut. The wound is not cleaned; other bacteria begin to grow, consuming the oxygen at the site and blocking off blood flow and oxygen. Suddenly, the spore, like a seed, opens, liberating an actively growing cell. The cell divides, and the population of C. tetani *grows. These cells start producing tetanus toxin. What will be the fate of the woodsman?*

FACTORS REQUIRED FOR *C. TETANI* GROWTH IN THE BODY

C. tetani is an obligate anaerobe, meaning it can grow only if oxygen is absent from the environment. Therefore, under most conditions, *C. tetani* cannot grow in the body, since most tissues get a rich supply of oxygen from the blood.

However, under some conditions, such as a deep puncture wound in the foot, oxygen can rapidly be depleted due to tissue damage that restricts blood flow and bacterial growth in the wound that uses up the remaining oxygen. Under these conditions the bacterial spores will germinate, and *C. tetani* will begin to grow. Since this microbe cannot metabolize most sugars, it depends on proteins and fats from the surrounding damaged

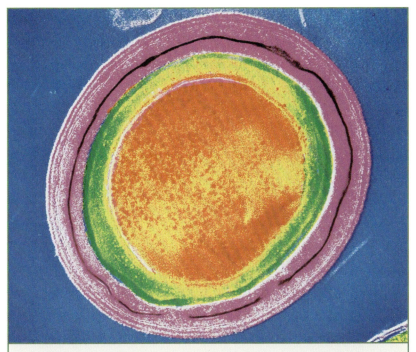

Figure 3.1   False-color transmission electron micrograph (TEM) of a *C. tetani* bacterial spore.   (CNRI/Photo Researchers, Inc.)

tissues for growth and reproduction. In wounds where *C. tetani* grows, the lack of oxygen prevents cells of the immune system from functioning, so the bacterium has to do relatively little to avoid the host immune response.

  C. tetani is adept at colonizing wounds, and it therefore seems likely that this microbe produces other factors that may assist it in establishing infection. For example, the protein tetanolysin is produced by *C. tetani*. It has been speculated that this protein may assist *C. tetani* in the colonization of anaerobic sites in the body by breaking open red blood cells, thereby providing the bacterium with a source of iron and other nutrients. Also, a collagenase, a type of enzyme that breaks down tissue by destroying the human protein collagen, is encoded by a gene present in *C. tetani*. This collagenase enzyme may provide nutrients for the bacterial cell, and it may help maintain the anaerobic environment essential for *C. tetani* to thrive. Other factors that assist this microbe in causing disease probably include **proteases**, enzymes that degrade proteins to amino acids, which are then used as nutrients for the microbe. It is likely that further research will lead to the discovery of additional proteins or other factors that assist *C. tetani* in setting up housekeeping in wounds.

TETANOSPASMIN

The symptoms of tetanus appear to be caused entirely, or almost entirely, by the tetanus toxin, tetanospasmin. This was demonstrated as far back as the late 1800s, when it was found that a bacteria-free solution from a *C. tetani* culture could induce in animals the same symptoms as infection with the microbe itself. The gene encoding this toxin is found only in the **genome** (the entire set of genetic instructions of an organism) of strains of *C. tetani* that cause tetanus. The toxic dose of tetanospasmin is very low—about 165 ng for a person weighing about 150 pounds (68 kg). This is about 2.5 parts per trillion, and would be about equal to the weight of 1/20th of a small grain of sand.[35] This dose is so low that an immune response to tetanospasmin does not occur during a natural infection. Tetanus toxin is the second most potent toxin known to humans, surpassed only by botulinum toxin, which is produced by strains of *Clostridium botulinum*. (Botulinum toxin is three to four times more toxic than tetanus toxin.) It has been estimated that about 80 million tetanus toxin molecules would be sufficient to kill a mouse; it would require about 30 billion times more molecules of cyanide to kill a mouse.[36]

It is generally accepted that tetanus toxin is released only when *C. tetani* cells break open. This has implications for the treatment of tetanus. For example, it may be critical to give tetanus immunoglobulin prior to the infusion of antibiotics to prevent excess toxin from being released once the antibiotic destroys the bacterial cells. However, the recently completed genome sequence of *C. tetani* identified a number of genes that encode secretion-system proteins, which can move other proteins out of the cell. This leaves open the possibility that the toxin may be exported by living cells, since these secretion proteins could play a role in toxin transfer out of the bacterial cell. If this is the case, it would be less likely to matter whether tetanus immunoglobulin or antibiotics were given first. Better understanding of these mechanisms may have an impact on treatment of tetanus in the future.

REGULATION OF TETANUS TOXIN PRODUCTION

It requires a substantial amount of energy for a cell to produce proteins, so it makes sense that these proteins will only be produced when it is advantageous to the microbe. This logic applies to genes that encode **virulence factors**, which are proteins that assist a microbe in causing disease. It makes sense for the organism to express these proteins only when the microbe is inside a host, for example, and not when the microbe is lying in the soil.

The most prominent virulence factor for *C. tetani* is tetanus toxin (tetanospasmin). Tetanospasmin is encoded by the *tet*X gene, which is located on a small circular section of DNA called a **plasmid**. In addition to the *tet*X gene, this plasmid contains genes that regulate tetanus toxin production, including *tet*R, which encodes the TetR protein.

TetR is the best-studied factor that controls the production of tetanus toxin. This protein helps determine whether the tetanus toxin gene, *tet*X, will be transcribed. **Transcription** is the process of converting information in DNA to another molecule called **messenger RNA**; this messenger RNA is then converted to a protein. So the TetR protein directly determines whether the tetanus toxin will be produced. More specifically, the TetR protein does this by acting as a **sigma factor**. Sigma factors are part of the transcription machinery in the cell; they help the transcription machinery (RNA polymerase) determine which genes to transcribe. In this case, TetR assists the transcription

TETANUS VERSUS BOTULINUM

Tetanus toxin has been documented to cause disease only when it is produced in an infected wound. Ingested tetanus toxin has not been reported to cause tetanus. Toxin produced by *C. botulinum* is chemically very similar to tetanus toxin, yet botulism normally results from eating food that is contaminated with botulinum toxin. The primary difference between the toxins appears to be the way they are released from the bacterial cell. Tetanus toxin is released from the cell as a single protein, and becomes activated when that protein is split into a heavy and light chain, and those two chains are joined back together.

The active botulism toxin protein also consists of a heavy and light chain, and is almost identical in size to the tetanus toxin protein. However, unlike tetanus toxin, botulism toxin is normally released from the bacterial cell in a complex with other proteins. This complex is large (about six times the size of the botulism toxin itself) and the complex apparently protects the toxin from the low pH and digestive enzymes in the stomach and intestines. When tested in the laboratory, the botulism toxin itself was quickly broken down by stomach acid, and rapidly degraded when exposed to digestive enzymes. However, in the natural protein complex, the

machinery in recognizing and transcribing *tet*X.[38] Helping to confirm the regulatory role of TetR, experiments have shown that *C. tetani* that produce more TetR protein also produce more tetanus toxin.

Sigma factors like TetR are, in turn, frequently controlled by **sensor proteins** that the bacterial cell uses to monitor environmental changes. In other pathogens, environmental factors such as temperature changes, the presence or absence of nutrients, and other factors can lead to the expression of virulence factors. It is not yet clear what external triggers activate TetR,

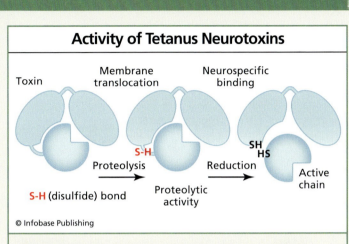

Activity of Tetanus Neurotoxins

Toxin — Membrane translocation — Neurospecific binding

S-H — Proteolysis — Reduction — Active chain

S-H (disulfide) bond — Proteolytic activity — SH HS

© Infobase Publishing

Figure 3.2   The activation of tetanus toxin requires the separation of the two parts of the toxin. This occurs in a nerve cell.

botulism toxin was very stable in the presence of either acid or digestive enzymes, which is probably the reason botulism results from consuming food. Tetanus toxin is not protected by a complex of other proteins, so it is probably destroyed in the gastrointestinal tract before it can do any damage. This likely explains why tetanus cases only arise from wound infections.[37]

but *C. tetani* does possess sensor proteins that may relay environmental signals and activate TetR, leading to the production of the tetanus toxin.

ACTIVATION OF TETANUS TOXIN

The tetanus toxin, tetanospasmin, is inactive when initially released from the bacterial cell. The toxin is a relatively large protein, with a molecular weight of approximately 150,000 **daltons** (a dalton is the weight of one hydrogen atom). Following its release from the bacterial cell, the tetanus toxin is cut by a bacterial or human protease **enzyme** into two sections, a heavy and a light chain. The heavy chain is approximately 100,000 daltons; the light chain is 50,000 daltons. The heavy and light chains reassemble, joined by a sulfur-sulfur bond, into an active toxin. If the sulfur-sulfur bond is removed before the toxin reaches a nerve cell, the toxin is inactivated.

TRANSPORT OF TETANUS TOXIN TO THE SPINAL CORD

The toxin, once released by the bacterial cell, is transported in the tissues or the bloodstream until it reaches a nerve-muscle junction, or synapse. At the nerve-muscle junction the heavy chain of the toxin binds to one or more specific proteins on the surface of the nerve cell, and to other molecules located in the nerve cell membrane.[39] (At least one

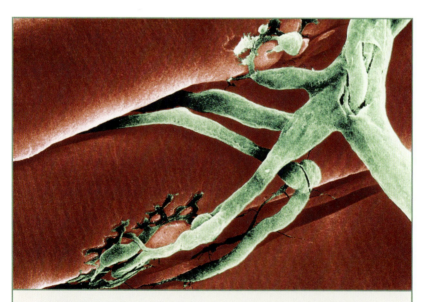

Figure 3.3 Colored scanning electron micrograph (SEM) of the junctions between a nerve cell (green) and a muscle fiber (red). Such junctions are known as synapses. (Don W. Fawcett/Photo Researchers, Inc.)

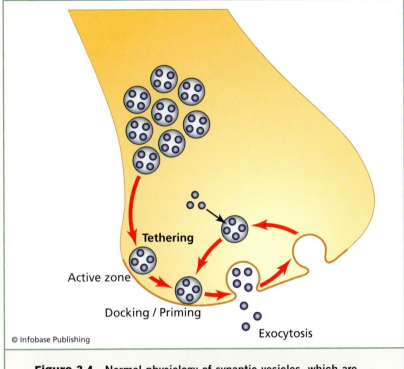

Figure 3.4 Normal physiology of synaptic vesicles, which are involved in neurotransmission. Tetanus toxin inhibits the tethering step, which prevents the synaptic vesicle from functioning. (The small, blue balls represent neurotransmitters)

protein on the nerve cells has been identified as a possible binding protein for tetanus toxin [Thy-1]. However, mice lacking this protein are still sensitive to tetanus toxin, indicating that other proteins likely play a role in toxin binding as well.[40]) Presumably these specific molecules are found only on the surface of nerve cells, which is why tetanus toxin interacts only with those cells.

Once bound to the outside of a nerve, tetanus toxin is taken inside the cell. The heavy chain of tetanus toxin is responsible for internalization. It appears that the heavy chain enters a **synaptic vesicle** (a membrane bound compartments in nerve cells containing neurotransmitters), which then joins with the plasma membrane of the nerve cells.

The intact toxin, located in a vesicle, is then transported to neurons in the spinal cord by hijacking a natural process called **retrograde transport**. Normally, this process acts like a conveyer belt to move molecules from the peripheral nerves to the spinal cord; it is required for nerve cell growth and survival. Once in the spinal cord, tetanus toxin exits the motor neuron and enters at the synapse of an inhibitory neuron. This is a nerve cell that normally functions to prevent transmission of nerve impulses in motor neurons. Tetanus

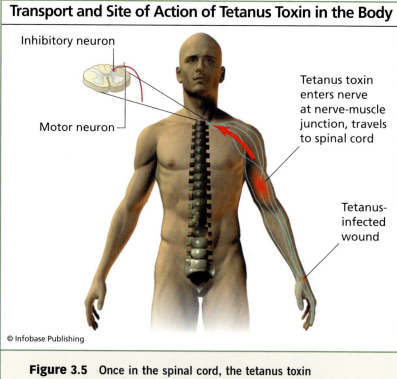

Transport and Site of Action of Tetanus Toxin in the Body

Inhibitory neuron

Motor neuron

Tetanus toxin enters nerve at nerve-muscle junction, travels to spinal cord

Tetanus-infected wound

© Infobase Publishing

Figure 3.5   Once in the spinal cord, the tetanus toxin inactivates inhibitory neurons, leading to continuous muscle contractions, since the motor neurons can now constantly transmit signals to the muscles.

toxin inhibits these inhibitory nerves, causing the severe uncontrolled muscle contractions that are the hallmark of this disease.[41]

Evidence that tetanus toxin operates on the spinal cord was known for a long time. In 1894, Warbasse, for example, reported the work of others in which frogs were infected with *C. tetani*. The frogs showed typical tetanus symptoms when they were inoculated with the microbe. If the spinal cords of the frogs were then destroyed, the tetanus symptoms were alleviated.[42] This indicated that the toxin operated on the spinal cord.

ACTION OF TOXIN INSIDE THE NERVES

Once inside the inhibitory neuron, the light chain of the tetanus toxin needs to separate from the heavy chain and move into the cytoplasm in order to become active. This movement appears to be triggered by a lowering of the pH once the toxin gets inside the cell, which changes the shape of the toxin and allows both the heavy and light chains to insert into the membrane of the compartment surrounding the toxin. Consequently, ion channels form in the membrane, and the sulfur-sulfur bond holding the light and heavy chains together is removed. This activates the light chain, which then enters the cytoplasm.

The light chain of the tetanus toxin then chops off a portion of a nerve cell protein, called **synaptobrevin** (a protein required for transmission of nerve impulses). This prevents the nerve cell synaptic vesicle from docking with the nerve cell membrane. As a result, a packet of neurotransmitters cannot be released from the cell, and no inhibitory signals are produced by the nerve. The result is continuous, painful muscle contraction. Once the toxin has done damage to the nerve cell, weeks or months may be required to fully re-establish damaged nerve-muscle junctions.[43] Consequently, the recovery period from tetanus frequently takes several weeks to months once treatment is complete.

4

How Is Tetanus Treated?

Recently a patient had surgery to repair a ruptured Achilles tendon. This person was an immigrant to Canada, and apparently had no previous tetanus vaccinations. He had pain and stiffness in his neck and shoulders five days following the surgery, and went to the hospital. His condition worsened, and he was ultimately treated for tetanus, which apparently resulted from infection of his surgical wound. He was in intensive care for six weeks, had five more weeks of treatment in the hospital, and then underwent additional weeks of rehabilitation. Ultimately, the patient had an almost full recovery. This example illustrates that tetanus spores are widespread in the environment, even in very clean areas like a hospital. It also shows the importance of tetanus vaccination in preventing disease.[44]

Once a person develops symptoms of tetanus treatment is difficult, because nothing can be done to reverse the effects of the toxin that has entered the nerve cells. In addition, since the toxin is an enzyme (a protein catalyst), it can repeatedly interfere with the ability of the nerve to transmit impulses. Once tetanus toxin has damaged the nerves, it requires several weeks for the synthesis of new nerve terminals, and that is why recovery following tetanus takes a good deal of time. However, even though recovery is slow, it is normally complete unless there are complications. Complications are common, though, since the treatment of tetanus is prolonged and intensive. These additional medical complications include everything from weight loss from the severe exertion caused by the intense muscle spasms associated with tetanus, to fractures and muscle damage caused by the contractions, to pneumonia as a consequence of mechanical ventilation to assist breathing.

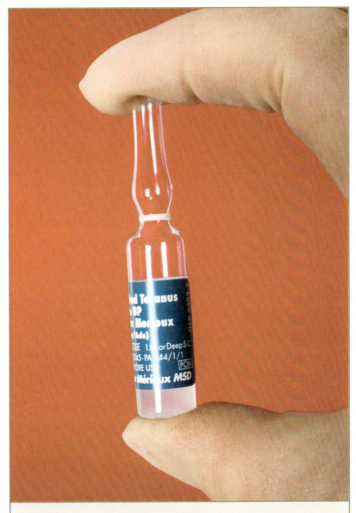

Figure 4.1 Gloved fingers holding an ampoule of tetanus toxoid, a treatment for tetanus. (Claire Paxton & Jacqui Farrow/Photo Researchers, Inc.)

In spite of the difficulty of treating tetanus, major advances in intensive care have dramatically improved the survival rate for tetanus patients. In the United States in the 1940s, the survival rate for people with tetanus was about 10 percent.

Currently the mortality rate is 5 to 10 percent, a dramatic improvement in treatment outcome.

Tetanus treatment consists primarily of the following three steps:[45]

- Ensuring that any circulating toxin that hasn't reached the nerves is neutralized. This is achieved by giving patients an injection of tetanus immunoglobulin. As described previously, this is a cocktail of antibodies from people who have been vaccinated with tetanus toxoid. These antibodies will bind to circulating tetanus toxin and prevent the toxin from entering the nerve cells. The tetanus immunoglobulin circulates in the blood for at least three weeks, so repeated treatment is usually not needed. In some countries, the immunoglobulin preparation comes from horses. This preparation is less expensive but is more likely to cause side effects, since some people are allergic to proteins found in horse serum.

- Ensuring that no new toxin is produced. This is achieved in two ways. First, antibiotics such as metronidazole and penicillin are given to destroy the bacteria still present in the body. Second, obvious wounds are thoroughly cleaned to ensure that any pockets of anaerobic tissue are eliminated, since these are sites where *C. tetani* could grow.

- Treating symptoms of the disease. Intense spastic muscle contractions are controlled through the use of muscle relaxants. Breathing difficulty is treated with mechanical ventilation, in many cases requiring a tracheotomy. Since the smallest disturbance can trigger a muscular spasm, patients are normally kept in a dark, quiet room. Patients typically require feeding with a gastric tube or intravenous line, since they are unable to open their jaws, chew, or swallow. Once a patient's muscle contractions and airway are stabilized, there is still potential for the development of heart irregularities that could cause death. In some cases pacemakers are required to restore normal function. Because of the length of treatment, special beds are often used for tetanus patients in order to prevent bedsores and nerve damage.

In one study, patients took one to seven months, depending on the severity of symptoms, before they were able to return to work following treatment for tetanus. The length of the recovery period demonstrates the severity of the disease. Despite the serious symptoms that patients in this study developed, 12 of the 50 individuals subsequently failed to complete their immunizations for tetanus, meaning they likely would not be protected against a future tetanus infection. At many hospitals vaccination against tetanus is part of the treatment regime for anyone who has developed tetanus.

Physicians may try to treat potential cases of tetanus proactively by identifying individuals who may be infected and, before they show symptoms, vaccinating them and administering tetanus immunoglobulin. In these cases doctors may attempt to determine whether a person has had a recent tetanus shot—either from the patient's medical history or based on a diagnostic test. They may also take special care with wounds particularly prone to developing tetanus (for example, those contaminated with soil or fecal material).

In addition to the physical symptoms of the disease, a substantial fraction of patients (perhaps one-third), particularly those who had severe symptoms, develop psychological problems. These often wane quickly after the tetanus is treated. For some people, though, the symptoms last substantially longer than one year. Some of the anxiety leading to psychological symptoms was associated with recalling the excruciating pain of tetanus spasms, or the fear of being removed from the respirator and being unable to breathe. Therefore, psychological support may be an important part of treating tetanus as well.[46]

Fortunately, the dramatic improvement in intensive care in developed countries has greatly improved the likelihood of

HISTORICAL TREATMENTS FOR TETANUS

425 B.C.: Hippocrates described the application of soothing plasters.

First century: Aretaeus, the Cappadocian, described the treatment of tetanus by bleeding: ". . . we must open the vein at the elbow, taking especial care with respect to the binding of the arm, that it be rather loose; and as to the incision, that it be performed in a gentle and expeditious manner, as these things provoke spasms; and take away a moderate quantity at first, yet not so as to induce fainting and coldness."[47]

1859: Luigi Vella used curare, an agent that paralyzes the muscles, to treat tetanus. This treatment is sometimes used today, particularly in the developing world, although the dose that eases symptoms is close to the dose that can cause death.

1897: F. Dennis,[48] a professor of surgery at Bellevue Hospital Medical College, described the state of the art for treating tetanus. Tetanus immunoglobulin had just become available and was the first really effective therapy for tetanus. He also indicated that wounds should be thoroughly cleaned, although the methods described seem a bit primitive. For example, it was recommended that

> In attempts to render the wound aseptic, all scabs should be removed and at once burned, since the bacilli have been found in these crusts. The wound underneath the scabs should be thoroughly disinfected. For purposes of disinfection . . . a 5% solution of carbolic acid or 1/1000 solution of bichloride of mercury to which is added a 1/2% solution of hydrochloric acid, will kill the spores in 10 minutes. . . . cautery has also been suggested as a means of destroying the microbes,

Figure 4.2   Pressure chambers like these were once tried (without much success) as a treatment for tetanus. (Bettmann/Corbis)

but this kind of treatment must be used under the influence of an anesthetic. . . . The elimination of the poison is the next step to consider in the treatment. The toxines [*sic*] of tetanus are chiefly eliminated by diuresis [through the urine]. To best utilize this channel of elimination, the imbibition of large quantities of fluid is indicated.

1898: Direct injection of tetanus antitoxin into the brain, a technique that was discredited a few years later.

(continues)

(continued)

1915–1926: Development of tetanus toxoid vaccine by several scientists, including Lowenstein, Eisler, Ramon, Descombey, and Zoller. Of these scientists, Ramon is generally credited with playing the most important role in developing the vaccine.

1968: Trial using a hyperbaric chamber (typically used for treating divers who surface too quickly) to treat severe cases of tetanus. The rationale was that, since *C. tetani* was an anaerobe, additional oxygen in the body might hinder the growth of the organism, and possibly counteract the effects of the toxin. Unfortunately, treatment in the chamber in some cases appeared to exacerbate the spasms associated with tetanus. Overall, the results were not encouraging, with six of the eight treated patients dying of tetanus.[49]

surviving tetanus infection. Future advances in prevention and treatment—including methods that counteract the effects of the toxin, even after it has reached the nerves—should reduce the number of cases and the severity of disease when it occurs. Much work still needs to be done to extend vaccine coverage and enhance the effectiveness of inexpensive treatment in developing countries.

5

How Is Tetanus Prevented?

"As a child, I was more afraid of tetanus shots than, for example, Dracula."
—Dave Barry[50]

In the late 1990s, a nine-day-old infant was brought into a hospital in Montana. The baby girl had suddenly become unable to nurse, and had difficulty opening her jaws. The child's condition quickly worsened, and she experienced strong muscle spasms and breathing difficulty. Ultimately the infant was placed on a mechanical ventilator and was hospitalized for three weeks of intensive medical care to treat a serious case of tetanus. The baby's mother had never had a tetanus vaccination. Following the birth, the baby's umbilical cord was covered with nonsterile clay. This clay may have either been the source of the bacteria, or may have allowed anaerobic conditions to develop in the cord, which favored growth of *C. tetani*. In spite of this incident, seven months later, the infant still had not been vaccinated against tetanus. This case shows, once again, the importance of tetanus vaccination. Maternal antibodies from vaccinated mothers are transferred to the infant during pregnancy and breastfeeding so that the baby is protected from the disease. All recent cases of neonatal tetanus in the United States have occurred in infants whose mothers were not vaccinated or were inadequately vaccinated. This case also demonstrates the prolonged and intensive treatment required to save a patient who has contracted the disease.[51]

The primary method for preventing tetanus is ensuring that individuals are vaccinated. The vaccine consists of the tetanus toxin, isolated from

C. tetani cultures, which is inactivated with a combination treatment using the disinfectant formaldehyde and the amino acid lysine, held at a slightly elevated temperature for several weeks. The inactivated toxin is called tetanus toxoid. The exact mechanism by which tetanus toxin is inactivated during the production of the vaccine is not completely understood, although recent work has provided a partial understanding of the differences between the functional, deadly toxin and the harmless toxoid.

Formaldehyde cross-links proteins and analysis of the toxoid shows that cross-linking of the tetanospasmin protein does occur following treatment with this chemical. This is probably

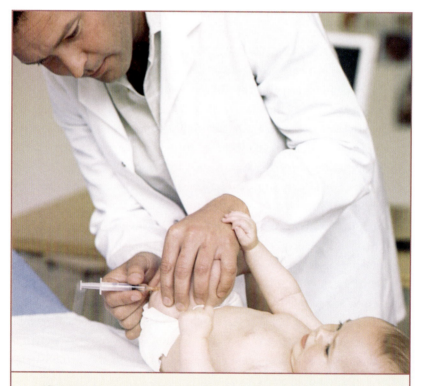

Figure 5.1 Four-month-old baby girl having a vaccine injected into her leg from a syringe. Vaccination is the best way to prevent tetanus. (Ian Hooton/Photo Researchers, Inc.)

critical, since separation of the toxin's light chain from its heavy chain is required for toxin activity in the cell, and cross-linking would likely prevent that separation. In addition, the formaldehyde and lysine alter some of the amino acids in the toxin, likely also contributing to the inactivation of the toxin.[52] Once the chemical treatment is completed, the formaldehyde and lysine are removed from the preparation. The toxoid is then tested in animals to verify that it is no longer toxic, and to determine its ability to promote an immune response. Doses of the toxoid are standardized and then incorporated into a vaccine. Some of the vaccine preparations contain only tetanus toxoid (TT), some contain both tetanus toxoid and diphtheria toxoid (Td), and some contain tetanus and diphtheria toxoid along with antigens from *Bordetella pertussis*, the causative agent of whooping cough (DTaP or DTP).

Since tetanus spores are widely distributed in nature, and are so resistant to destruction, it is likely that the tetanus vaccination will always be part of medical treatment. Some pathogens can be eliminated as a disease threat through vaccination and other health measures. This particularly applies to those, like the smallpox virus, that live only in humans and don't survive for long periods in the environment. However, because *C. tetani* can survive for decades in the soil, and because many animals besides humans can be infected with this microbe, it is unlikely that this pathogen will ever be eliminated from the environment. Therefore, people who haven't been vaccinated will likely always be at risk for infection.

The current vaccine schedule in the United States consists of six injections between birth and 12 years of age, followed up with booster injections every 10 years thereafter. Normally, the vaccine that is administered in childhood is called DTaP, which confers immunity to diphtheria, tetanus, and pertussis. After the childhood shots are given, booster shots consisting of tetanus toxoid and diphtheria toxoid are used. A detailed vaccination schedule, including that for DtaP, is given in Figure 5.2.

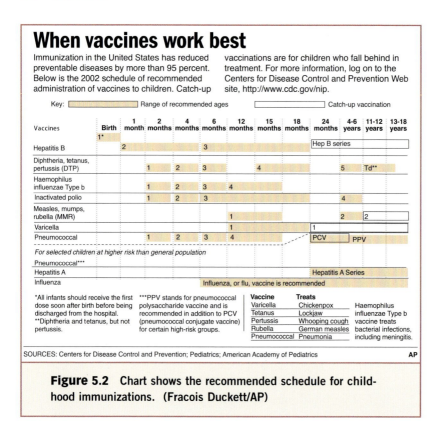

When vaccines work best

Immunization in the United States has reduced preventable diseases by more than 95 percent. Below is the 2002 schedule of recommended administration of vaccines to children. Catch-up vaccinations are for children who fall behind in treatment. For more information, log on to the Centers for Disease Control and Prevention Web site, http://www.cdc.gov/nip.

Key: [Range of recommended ages]   [Catch-up vaccination]

Vaccines	Birth	1 month	2 months	4 months	6 months	12 months	15 months	18 months	24 months	4-6 years	11-12 years	13-18 years
Hepatitis B	1*	2			3				Hep B series			
Diphtheria, tetanus, pertussis (DTP)			1	2	3		4			5	Td**	
Haemophilus influenzae Type b			1	2	3	4						
Inactivated polio			1	2	3					4		
Measles, mumps, rubella (MMR)						1				2	2	
Varicella						1			1			
Pneumococcal			1	2	3	4			PCV	PPV		

For selected children at higher risk than general population

Pneumococcal***												
Hepatitis A									Hepatitis A Series			
Influenza				Influenza, or flu, vaccine is recommended								

*All infants should receive the first dose soon after birth before being discharged from the hospital.
**Diphtheria and tetanus, but not pertussis.

***PPV stands for pneumococcal polysaccharide vaccine and is recommended in addition to PCV (pneumococcal conjugate vaccine) for certain high-risk groups.

Vaccine	Treats	
Varicella	Chickenpox	Haemophilus influenzae Type b vaccine treats bacterial infections, including meningitis.
Tetanus	Lockjaw	
Pertussis	Whooping cough	
Rubella	German measles	
Pneumococcal	Pneumonia	

SOURCES: Centers for Disease Control and Prevention; Pediatrics; American Academy of Pediatrics   AP

Figure 5.2   Chart shows the recommended schedule for child-hood immunizations. (Fracois Duckett/AP)

VACCINE SAFETY

Minor side effects from the tetanus toxoid vaccine are fairly common. A majority of patients in several studies reported pain, redness, or swelling at the site of the injection, which typically didn't last more than a day or two. A smaller percentage, ranging from 2 percent to 16 percent, depending on the report, experienced a short-term systemic effect such as fever, headache, or muscle ache. In some sense, these mild reactions are actually a good sign. They indicate a strong immune response to the components in the vaccine, suggesting that a person with these reactions would be able to fend off an infection with *C. tetani*.

While no medical intervention is without some risks, perhaps the best way of evaluating the risk from a tetanus vaccine is to compare the likelihood of serious harm from taking the vaccine to the likelihood of such harm from not taking the vaccine. Experts believe that there would be approximately 657 deaths per year from tetanus in the United States without vaccination.[53]

Researchers analyzed side effects linked to tetanus vaccine in the United States that were reported to the Vaccine Adverse Event Reporting System (VAERS) between 1991 and 1997.[54] In their analysis researchers from the Utah Department of Health, the Centers for Disease Control, and the Food and Drug Administration determined that two deaths occurred that *may* have been related to the 90 million doses of tetanus toxoid vaccine used during this period. But what would have happened had those doses not been dispensed? Based on the expected rate of two deaths from tetanus per million unvaccinated people, one would have expected 180 deaths. Considering that those two deaths were not definitely caused by the vaccination, the relative risk of death without the vaccine may well be greater than 90:1. The VAERS system collects voluntary reports of vaccine side effects from health care providers, patients, and others. Because the reports are not required, there is a concern that complications of vaccination may be underreported. However, another study indicated that very serious reactions, such as seizures, were very likely to be reported to VAERS, suggesting that most of the vaccine-associated deaths would have been reported.[55]

There have been several reports indicating that it is even safe to give the vaccine during pregnancy.[56] Because tetanus spores are widely distributed in the environment, the disease poses a substantial risk of death (even with excellent medical treatment), and it requires a long period of intensive medical care; therefore, the risks of getting the disease appear to be much greater than the risks associated with vaccination.

However, serious effects do sometimes occur for almost every widely used medical treatment. To provide a mechanism for compensating patients who have a serious adverse reaction to vaccination, the United States has established a National Vaccine Injury Compensation Program.[57] Currently, for tetanus toxoid vaccine, the serious complications for which compensation is available include:

- Anaphylaxis or anaphylactic shock within four hours of receiving the shot. This is a severe allergic reaction to the vaccine that can cause death as a result of airway blockage. Based on a study by scientists at research institutions and hospitals on the West Coast of the United States,[58] the risk of anaphylaxis for vaccines containing the tetanus toxoid is approximately two per million doses of vaccine. Although serious, if recognized quickly, this reaction can easily be treated in most medical settings.

- Brachial neuritis, a nervous system disorder that normally starts with a deep, severe pain in the arm and shoulder and eventually leads to muscle weakness in the upper body. Based on a study of side effects in infants, it appears that brachial neuritis occurs, in this age group at least, at a rate well below one case per 15 million doses.[59] In most patients, recovery from brachial neuritis begins within a month after symptoms appear, and 90 percent of patients had completely recovered after three years.[60]

There is both an element of personal benefit and social good involved in receiving vaccinations for communicable diseases. By having a large proportion of the population vaccinated, an epidemic would be less likely to spread, thereby offering additional protection both to those who are and those who are not vaccinated. An example of this type of disease would be diphtheria. Widespread vaccination reduces the risk of spread of this microbe in the population as a whole. Unlike diphtheria, tetanus is not contagious, and therefore vaccination for this disease is primarily a matter of personal protection.

ADJUVANTS AND VACCINES

One goal in modern vaccine development is to make vaccines single-shot treatments that lead to lifetime protection. Much of this work involves trying to trigger the immune system to respond to a harmless protein (like the tetanus toxoid in the tetanus vaccine) as if it were the most serious possible threat. The result would be a vigorous immune response, which might protect individuals for many decades.

To stimulate a stronger immune response to a vaccine, scientists sometimes use adjuvants, chemicals that enhance the body's reaction to a vaccine. Compounds as unusual as the tapioca used in pudding have been tested as adjuvants. Currently the only approved adjuvant in the United States for tetanus and other vaccines is alum (aluminum hydroxide). Alum is thought to work by binding to the tetanus toxoid, thereby causing the slower release of this protein in the body and lengthening the time the immune system is exposed to the vaccine. Alum may also improve the ability of cells of the immune system to take up vaccine components, and may also directly activate immune-system cells.[61] In spite of its widespread use in humans, alum is not the strongest adjuvant in animal tests, although it continues to be used because of its excellent safety record. Work is continuing on developing additional safe, and even more effective, adjuvants.

SKEPTICISM ABOUT VACCINATION

As the number of serious vaccine-preventable diseases has declined in developed countries, a perception has arisen that vaccines are more dangerous than the diseases they are intended to prevent. There have been claims that certain diseases are associated with specific vaccines. In many cases, these claims have not held up to scrutiny.

The tetanus vaccine is considered by health authorities to be one of the safest vaccines, for the following reasons:

- It consists of only one protein, the inactivated tetanus toxoid.

- It does not include dead, whole microbes, or living but weakened microbes.

Most people who choose not to get vaccinated against tetanus are opposed to all vaccines, rather than just this specific one. A recent report[62] by researchers at the Centers for Disease Control showed that objection to vaccination is a risk factor for tetanus. Since most adults have never seen a person with tetanus, a lack of awareness of the seriousness of the disease is one factor that may keep parents from vaccinating their children. Of 15 cases of tetanus in children reported between 1992 and 2000 in the United States, 12 occurred in children who had never been vaccinated because their parents objected to the vaccines; in one additional case (an infant), the mother had been vaccinated 18 years earlier but had received no recent vaccinations. In the remaining two children who had previously been vaccinated, the course of the disease was milder, with an average of two days of hospitalization. Among the unvaccinated children, the average stay in the hospital was 28 days.

NATURAL IMMUNITY TO TETANUS?

An infection with *C. tetani* apparently does not lead to protection against future infections with the organism, based on a number of case reports of individuals who developed tetanus twice. This is thought to be a consequence of the extremely high potency of the tetanus toxin, tetanospasmin, which is lethal in very small amounts, and the fact that the toxin is hidden away so quickly in the nerves that the immune system is unable to recognize and respond to it.

Despite those facts, there have been several reports of people with natural immunity to the toxin. In one example,[63] Ethiopian immigrants to Israel were tested for the presence of antibodies to tetanus toxin (a measure of immunity to the disease). Owing to the poor state of health care in Ethiopia, none of the immigrants had apparently ever seen a doctor, and none were thought to have received a tetanus vaccination. A total of 200 individuals were sampled, and 30 percent (61) of them had levels of antibody to tetanus toxin that are normally considered protective.

There have been other studies of unvaccinated individuals with similar findings. For example, 57 people living on the Galapagos Islands who indicated they had never received a tetanus vaccination were tested for antibodies to tetanus toxin. All had antibody levels that would normally be considered protective against the disease.[64] In another study, 59 adults from Brazil with no previous history of tetanus immunization were tested for antibodies to tetanus toxin. More than 25 percent of these individuals had antibodies against tetanus that would normally be considered protective.[65] (However, even if future work confirms natural immunity to tetanus, many people had not developed an immune response in these studies, and would not be protected from the disease. Therefore, this data should not have any bearing on the need for continued vaccination.)

It is unclear what the source of natural immunity might be, but it is thought that ingestion of *C. tetani* cells or spores might allow the immune system to recognize the organism, or the toxin it produces, as it passes through the gastrointestinal tract (although conditions in the intestines would not sustain growth of the organism). Support for this argument comes from serological surveys of native Brazilians from an area where no tetanus has been reported. None of the 30 individuals tested had evidence of any antibody response to tetanus toxin. Further support for the possibility of some level of natural immunity comes from the idea that animals can become immune to tetanus by injections of sublethal doses of the toxin, followed by gradually increasing doses, until they eventually can withstand a toxin dose that would otherwise be deadly.

6

Continuing Concerns and Current Status of Tetanus

In the late 1990s a middle-aged man checked into a hospital complaining of back pain. The patient had abscesses in his thighs at sites where he had recently injected heroin. Initially he had tried treating those sores himself by cutting them open with a pocketknife. Not surprisingly, his condition worsened. As part of his workup in the hospital, a measurement was made of his immune response to tetanus toxin. It was found to be at a level that normally correlates with protection from this disease. In spite of his positive immune status, he was treated with tetanus immunoglobulin and antibiotics. Eventually he developed muscle spasms, stopped breathing, and had to be resuscitated. During this time, the lack of oxygen caused brain injury that ultimately led to his death. This case shows that while tetanus vaccination is normally protective, there may be some special circumstances in which even immunization does not provide an absolute guarantee against infection.[66]

TETANUS IN INJECTION DRUG USERS

Tetanus has been identified as a health concern for injection drug users since the 1870s when it was first reported in addicts who injected morphine under the skin, or subcutaneously.[67] Even today tetanus is more common among injection drug users than among the general population. In the United States, between 1998 and 2000, 15 percent of tetanus cases occurred in injection drug users.[68] An abnormally high number of cases of tetanus in injection drug users has also been reported in

other countries. For example, 25 tetanus cases were identified in the United Kingdom from July 2003 to September
2004. Information was available on drug use for 21 of these
individuals, and 17 of them had a history of heroin use, specifically involving "skin popping," (injecting just under the
skin) or injecting into the muscles. For 20 of these individuals, tetanus immunization records were available. According
to the records, nine of the 20 had never been vaccinated, and
only one patient who had a complete series of tetanus shots
developed severe tetanus symptoms.[69]

The source of tetanus, at least in some cases, has been the
heroin itself. Tetanus spores could potentially be introduced
into the heroin at a number of steps between harvest and
injection. Apparently, skin-popping may create an appropriate anaerobic environment for the growth of C. tetani, while
injecting heroin directly into the veins may not.

TETANUS IN VACCINATED INDIVIDUALS

People with up-to-date vaccinations for tetanus are almost
completely protected against it. Estimates are that only four
cases of tetanus occur per 100 million vaccinated individuals.[70] In the rare cases that individuals who are current with
their vaccinations develop tetanus, it may be due to variations
in genes involved in immunity. The individuals may not have
developed high levels of antibodies against the tetanus toxin. In
other cases, even with high levels of antibodies, a small number
of individuals are not protected from tetanus.[71]

In some circumstances, this may be due to the production of ineffective antibodies. This was demonstrated in a case
in which a person with a level of antibody about 20 times
greater than normally needed to confer protection from disease developed a severe case of tetanus. Injection of antibodies
(serum) from this patient into mice did not protect the mice
from tetanus infection and death.[72] (In a person with protective antibodies, an injection of serum would protect the mice
against infection and death.)

In other cases, the amount of toxin produced from a wound infected with *C. tetani* may be so great as to overwhelm the immune response, even if the person has functional antibodies. Therefore, even in individuals with a history of current tetanus vaccination, health authorities remind physicians to keep in mind the need to treat all patients who show symptoms of tetanus.

TETANUS IN THE ELDERLY POPULATIONS IN DEVELOPED COUNTRIES

Only about 50 percent of people over 50 in the United States had been adequately vaccinated against tetanus, based on a survey reported in 2002.[73] Tetanus immunity (based on circulating antibody levels) exists in more than 80 percent of people under 40, but only about 25 percent of people over 70.[74] One reason is the poor rates of vaccination in the older age group, but an additional factor is the diminished response to vaccination in the elderly. As people age, their immune system becomes less able to develop antibodies following vaccination.

Because of lower vaccination rates and waning immunity, the elderly are one of the highest risk populations for tetanus. In 1998–2000, in the United States, the rate of tetanus infection in those over 60 was about 1 per 3 million individuals, a rate about twice that of the U.S. population as a whole. During this period 75 percent of deaths from tetanus in the United States were among patients older than 60 years. As a further illustration, in 2004 there were two tetanus deaths in the United States. An 85-year-old woman with a single tetanus vaccination 50 years earlier was one of the patients; the other was a 78-year-old woman with a history of diabetes and no history of tetanus vaccination.[75]

TETANUS IN IMMUNOCOMPROMISED INDIVIDUALS

People with compromised immune systems (kidney dialysis patients, HIV-infected individuals, and others) frequently respond poorly to vaccinations. For example, in a study of 71 kidney dialysis patients in Germany, researchers from

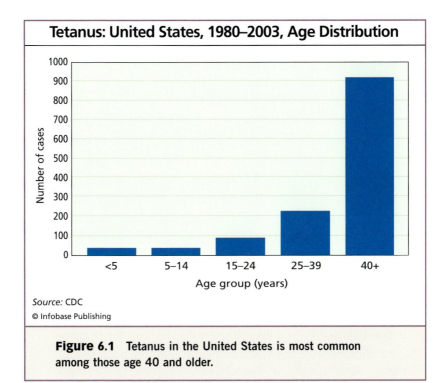

Tetanus: United States, 1980–2003, Age Distribution

Source: CDC

© Infobase Publishing

Figure 6.1   Tetanus in the United States is most common among those age 40 and older.

the University of Lubek found that fewer than half of these individuals had high enough antibody levels to be considered protected against tetanus. In the 40 patients who had low antibody levels against tetanus, only 38 percent (15) responded to a dose of the vaccine and produced protective levels of antibodies, while the majority (25 patients or 63 percent) did not respond to the vaccine. In contrast, up to 96 percent of healthy individuals respond to tetanus vaccine by producing protective levels of antibodies against tetanus.[76]

Similarly, individuals who were severely immunocompromised as a consequence of HIV infection had a low level of response to tetanus vaccination. In studies conducted at two different hospitals in Europe, those individuals with the lowest counts of immune system cells (corresponding to the greatest immune deficiency) had the poorest response to the vaccine.[77]

These results suggest that new strategies for the timing of booster vaccinations, or perhaps even a new vaccine formulation, may be needed to adequately protect immunocompromised individuals.

RELIGIOUS OR PHILOSOPHICAL OBJECTIONS TO TETANUS VACCINATION

Tetanus occurs almost exclusively in people who have not received an appropriately timed series of tetanus shots. In many countries, this is because suitable medical care is not available. However, in most developed countries, when individuals are not vaccinated it is primarily because they have religious or other objections to vaccination.

A report published in 2002 by researchers at the Centers for Disease Control and Prevention indicated that from 1992 to 2000 there were 15 cases of tetanus reported in children less than 15 years of age in the United States. In 12 of the 15 cases, the children were not vaccinated because of the parents' religious or philosophical objection to vaccination. In six of the 12 cases where the children hadn't been vaccinated, they were members of an Amish community.[78] Since tetanus has been associated with fecal contamination of soil from animals, and since Amish people traditionally live on farms, they may be more exposed to tetanus, and less protected, than the general population of the United States.

TETANUS FOLLOWING NATURAL DISASTERS

The importance of tetanus vaccination becomes particularly apparent following natural disasters. Injury and the subsequent potential for tetanus infection may be widespread following a natural disaster. For example, tetanus was reported in the Banda Aceh region of Indonesia following the tsunami in 2004. Since tetanus treatment often requires intensive medical care, the conditions following the tsunami (lack of equipment, medical supplies, and unsanitary conditions) hampered proper medical treatment for individuals with tetanus.[79]

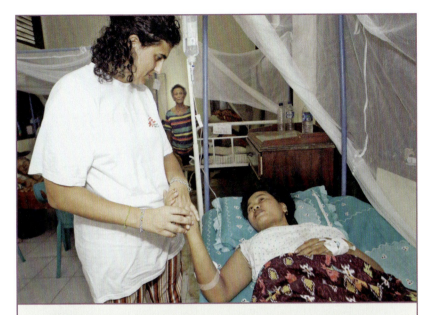

Figure 6.2   A doctor checks on a patient with tetanus after the December 26, 2004 tsunami that decimated large sections of southeast Asia. (Firdia Lisnawati/AP)

STATUS OF TETANUS IN THE UNITED STATES

In the United States the death rate, and the absolute number of deaths, due to tetanus dropped dramatically between 1900 and 2000. In 1900 there were 2,750 deaths in the United States due to tetanus (3.6 deaths per 100,000 population). Assuming a death rate of 90 percent, that would suggest the number of cases was approximately 3,055 (about 4.7 cases per 100,000 population).

At the start of widespread use of the tetanus vaccine, in the late 1940s, about 600 tetanus cases occurred per year in the United States (0.4 cases per 100,000 population) and about 540 deaths. Following the routine use of the vaccine in the 1940s, the number of cases and deaths dropped precipitously. In 2000 there were only 35 cases (0.01 cases per 100,000 population) and five deaths. Almost all of these reported cases and deaths occurred in individuals who had not had a tetanus vaccination within the previous 10 years.[81] Currently, it is estimated that in the United States alone vaccination for tetanus accounts for an estimated 657 lives saved annually. [82]

STATUS OF TETANUS IN DEVELOPING COUNTRIES

Worldwide the overall rate of tetanus infection is estimated to be about 180 cases per million people. In developing countries, the mortality rate can be as high as 300 per million people. In many of these countries, substantial progress has occurred in reducing the death toll from tetanus, particularly neonatal tetanus. The World Health Organization (WHO) estimated that nearly 800,000 infants died of neonatal tetanus in 1988. By 2000 it was estimated that the number of neonatal tetanus deaths had declined to 200,000.[83] Overall, widespread vaccination has substantially reduced the number of deaths from tetanus, saving an estimated 900,000 lives per year. However, tetanus still causes approximately 300,000 deaths per year. Vaccine coverage with three doses of DTP vaccine is in the 70 percent range in developing countries (for example, 66 percent

TRADITIONAL MEDICINE AND TETANUS

Despite the tremendous advances in medical science in recent decades, traditional cultural practices may still put many infants at risk for contracting tetanus. For example, in Pakistan, where clarified butter (called ghee) has been commonly used to cover an infant's umbilical cord, there is a high rate of neonatal tetanus. Investigation of cases of neonatal tetanus between 1989 and 1991 in Pakistan showed that dung was commonly used for heating the butter prior to its application.[80] Presumably, tetanus spores were present in the dung and at least some of those spores were transferred to the butter.

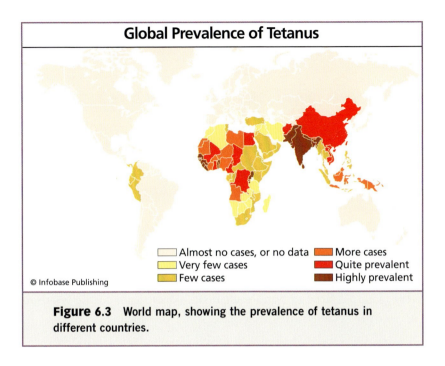

Figure 6.3 World map, showing the prevalence of tetanus in different countries.

in Africa and 69 percent in South East Asia).[84] There are several initiatives designed to increase the level of vaccination in the developing countries, including the Global Immunization Vision and Strategy (developed by the WHO and UNICEF) and the GAVI fund (a public-private foundation).

Unusual sources of tetanus exist in some developing countries. For example, in Nigeria several cases of tetanus have been reported following bites by poisonous snakes. In one report of four cases of tetanus following snakebite, two of the four individuals died—probably due in part to complications from the effects of both snake venom and tetanus.[85]

7
Future Prospects Regarding Tetanus

Botulinum toxin is widely used to treat medical conditions involving uncontrolled muscle contractions, such as cerebral palsy, and for cosmetic treatment of lines and wrinkles in the skin. Tetanus toxin is very closely related to botulinum toxin, which leads to the question of whether tetanus toxin may have some therapeutic usefulness. In spite of the similarity of the proteins, tetanus toxin and botulinum toxin have almost completely opposite effects, with tetanus toxin causing intense muscle contractions, and botulinum toxin preventing muscle contractions. Therefore, the two toxins aren't interchangeable. However, the ability of tetanus toxin to travel up the nerves to the spinal cord may some day provide a means of treating disorders of the central nervous system.

SINGLE-DOSE TETANUS VACCINATION

One major goal of the World Health Organization regarding tetanus is the development of a single-dose vaccine. Current vaccine schedules, requiring five or more separate shots, are frequently beyond the capacity of the medical system in developing countries. While the goal of a single shot to prevent tetanus has yet to be realized, progress has been made in new vaccine formulations that may eventually allow a single dose of a tetanus vaccine to confer life-long immunity.

One approach currently being tested is encapsulating the tetanus toxoid in **microspheres** (tiny beads consisting of material that is poorly degraded by the body), which then slowly release the antigen over a period of days, weeks, or months. As a result, the immune system is stimulated to respond to the tetanus toxoid for long periods of time, potentially generating life-long immunity.[86]

Another vaccination approach that is being tested is the expression of a portion of the harmless but immune-stimulating portion of the toxin gene in another bacterium. In one experiment, a fragment of the tetanus toxin gene was inserted into the genome of a bacterium called *Streptococcus gordonii*, which normally inhabits the oral cavity.

When mice were injected under their skin with a vaccine containing the modified microbe, a strong immune response to tetanus toxin developed in most of them. This bacterium protected over 80 percent of the treated mice against a dose of tetanus toxin 50 times larger than the amount that is normally fatal to unvaccinated mice.[87] This may be another strategy that could provide long-lasting protection against tetanus, perhaps with just a single shot.

INACTIVATING THE TOXIN ONCE IT REACHES THE NERVES

Once enough tetanus toxin reaches the nerves, currently available treatment may not be able to prevent symptoms from developing. Consequently, there has been interest in developing drugs that can enter the nerves and interfere with the action of the toxin. This work is still in the developmental stages, but there have been some encouraging reports in tests of small protein and other small molecule inhibitors of tetanus toxin.[88] To date, these molecules have only been used in test-tube experiments, but there is hope that these initial tests will ultimately lead to more effective treatments in people who have developed tetanus symptoms.

INSIGHTS FROM SEQUENCING THE COMPLETE GENOME OF *C. TETANI*

Since 1995 the ability to sequence whole bacterial genomes has revolutionized our understanding of many bacteria. The complete sequence of the genome of *C. tetani* was published in 2003. The analysis of this DNA sequence has revealed many previously unknown details about the biology of this organism.[89] These include insights into various proteins that might contribute to virulence, and a better understanding of the metabolism of the organism.

Virulence Factors

Most of the virulence factors in *C. tetani* are located on a circular molecule of DNA called a plasmid. This plasmid contains the tetanus toxin gene (*tet*X), a gene that regulates *tet*X (*tet*R), a gene (*col*T) that encodes a collagenase (an enzyme that degrades collagen, a protein in human tissue), other regulatory genes, and genes that encode proteins which transport other proteins across the cell membrane.

There are also several potential virulence factor genes located on the bacterial chromosome. These include a

Figure 7.1   False-color transmission electron micrograph of a plasmid of bacterial DNA. Plasmids contain many of the virulence factors in *C. tetani*. (Professor Stanley N. Cohen/Photo Researchers, Inc.)

SIMILAR GENETIC REGULATORY CIRCUITS IN OTHER RELATED PATHOGENS

Clostridium botulinum is closely related to *C. tetani*. This fact shows up in a number of ways, including how the two organisms determine whether to produce their respective toxins. Both *C. botulinum* and *C. tetani* have similar regulatory genes. The *C. tetani* gene called *tet*R has a counterpart in *C. botulinum* called *bot*R. Both of these genes regulate transcription of toxin genes, presumably in a similar manner. It is therefore possible that both organisms use similar cues (human body temperature, the presence of certain nutrients) to determine when it is appropriate to produce their toxins.[91]

tetanolysin, a hemolysin, and a fibronectin-binding protein. The chromosome also contains several genes that encode bacterial surface proteins that may be involved in binding human cells.

Other possible virulence factors in *C. tetani* have been identified by comparing its genome with that of *C. perfringens* (another clostridial pathogen that causes gangrene) and *C. acetobutylium* (a nonpathogenic clostridium). Approximately 700 of these factors are either present in both pathogens (199 genes) or found only in *C. tetani* (over 500 genes).[90] A number of **metalloproteases** (metal-requiring enzymes that degrade proteins) have been identified. These cut other proteins and require a metal, such as zinc, for activity; the tetanus toxin is an example of a metalloprotease, and some of these other enzymes may have as-yet-unidentified roles in the disease process.

Metabolism

In the analysis of the genome sequence, scientists discovered that *C. tetani* can use glucose for growth. Confirming previous work, they also found that this microbe does not have genes allowing it to metabolize the sugar sucrose or fructose. Another finding was that *C. tetani* has many genes which encode lipid-degrading enzymes, suggesting that lipids may be an important source of nutrients for it in the body. Further, according to the genome analysis, the microbe has many genes that produce amino acid-degrading enzymes. This confirms previous studies suggesting that amino acids are an important nutrient source for this organism.

In most bacteria, energy derived from nutrients like glucose is used to pump protons (H+ or hydrogen ions) across the membrane. These protons then serve as an energy reserve. When they are moved back across the membrane into the cell cytoplasm through specialized proteins, the cell is able to generate its primary energy storage chemical, **ATP**. Based on the genome sequence, it appears that *C. tetani* uses an alternate system. In this system numerous proteins act as sodium pumps, and ATP is generated when sodium atoms are brought back across the membrane.

A better understanding of the biology of this organism, as a result of the availability of the genome sequence, may open up new strategies for treating and preventing tetanus.

POTENTIAL FOR BETTER UNDERSTANDING TETANUS FROM GENETIC STUDIES

Some work has been done on the genetic manipulation of *Clostridium tetani*. In particular, one system for mutating the genome of the organism has been tested. It involved matings between another species of bacteria (*Enterococcus faecalis*), which contains a **transposon** (a section of DNA capable of moving into a new site in the genome, or into a new genome), and *C. tetani*. Following these matings, the transposon moved into multiple sites in the genome of *C. tetani*. During this process, insertion of the transposon usually disrupts a gene, causing a mutation. In genetics, scientists commonly study genes by mutating them and determining what effect this has on the organism in question. Further work along these lines may help scientists understand better how *C. tetani* causes disease.

In addition, some preliminary work has been done on introducing foreign DNA into *C. tetani*. In one report, *C. tetani* was transformed via **electroporation** (a technique where bacterial cells are mixed with DNA and treated with a high voltage pulse that causes the DNA to move into the cell) with a plasmid that encoded the regulatory gene *tet*R. Over-expression of this regulatory gene led to higher production of the tetanus toxin. This kind of experiment could lead to more efficient production of tetanus toxin, which might reduce the cost of making the tetanus vaccine. Further work on developing genetic techniques for *C. tetani* may reveal important insights into the biology of this organism, some of which may have value in advancing the clinical treatment of tetanus.[92] For example, a better understanding of the mechanisms that regulate tetanospasmin expression could lead to new therapies that could stop toxin production, and improve the survival rate for people with severe tetanus.

BETTER MANAGEMENT OF CLINICAL SIGNS OF DISEASE

The treatment of patients with tetanus has improved substantially, and the mortality rate has declined significantly. One of the remaining ways that treatment could be improved is by counteracting the effects tetanus has on the **autonomic nervous system**, the branch of the nervous system that is not under conscious control. One example of these dangerous effects is that *C. tetani* may induce cardiac arrest.

In addition, there have been very few controlled studies of various drugs and other interventions for treating tetanus.[93] More clinical studies would help more clearly define the best standards of practice for treating this disease, and potentially further reduce the death rate from tetanus.

In developing countries, advanced treatment is often not available, and the mortality rate for tetanus is still high. However, there have been some recent trials of inexpensive interventions, such as the use of magnesium sulphate to control seizures in patients with this disease.[94] Further work in the area of developing low-cost treatments for tetanus could help reduce the mortality from this disease in developing countries.

INSIGHTS REGARDING CELLULAR BIOLOGY

Tetanus toxin has been used help scientists better understand aspects of the basic biology of cells. For example, tetanus toxin has been used to understand how proteins leave cells, and the role of specific nerve cells in model organisms, like the fruit fly.

Use of tetanus toxin to block specific steps in protein trafficking

One way cells in our bodies communicate with one another is by releasing proteins, which then have an effect on other cells. Part of this process involves **SNARE proteins** (Soluble *NSF Accessory* protein *Receptors*; NSF stands for N-ethylmaleimide sensitive fusion proteins), which tether a packet of internal proteins to the cell membrane. Once the packet interacts with the cell membrane, these proteins can be released and affect other cells. Tetanus toxin acts like a "biochemical scalpel" in cleaving a specific SNARE protein (synaptobrevin, also called VAMP, for vesicle-associated membrane protein). Therefore, by exposing cells in culture to tetanus toxin, cell biologists can help identify the stages in cellular release of proteins.[95]

Expression of tetanus toxin to disable specific nerves

Modern genetic technology has led to the ability to do very sophisticated manipulation of organisms. For example, genetic tools have been developed to insert the tetanus toxin light chain gene into the genome of a number of organisms, including the fruit fly, *Drosophila melanogaster*. The tetanus toxin light chain is the part of the toxin that prevents the transmission of nerve impulses. The light chain normally requires the heavy chain (the other portion of the toxin) to get into the nerves. However, in this system the light chain is randomly inserted into the genome of the fruit fly, so it is produced directly inside nerve cells. Therefore, the heavy chain of the tetanus toxin is not required.

In this system, the tetanus toxin gene is engineered so it is part of a DNA fragment that also contains an **upstream activating sequence** that binds a yeast protein called GAL4. (Upstream activating sequences are located next to a gene. In the presence of the appropriate signals, those sequences activate transcription of the adjacent gene. The GAL4 protein is

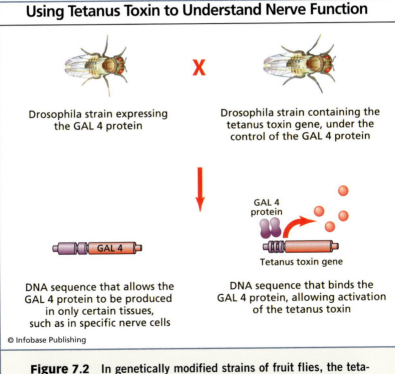

Using Tetanus Toxin to Understand Nerve Function

X

Drosophila strain expressing the GAL 4 protein

Drosophila strain containing the tetanus toxin gene, under the control of the GAL 4 protein

GAL 4

GAL 4 protein

Tetanus toxin gene

DNA sequence that allows the GAL 4 protein to be produced in only certain tissues, such as in specific nerve cells

DNA sequence that binds the GAL 4 protein, allowing activation of the tetanus toxin

© Infobase Publishing

Figure 7.2 In genetically modified strains of fruit flies, the tetanus toxin is produced in specific nerve cells, thereby destroying the function of those cells. In the figure above, the purple balls represent the GAL4 protein, and the red balls represent the tetanus toxin.

normally involved in the regulation of galactose metabolism in yeast, but in this system it has been adapted to regulate the tetanus toxin light chain gene.) The GAL4 gene, in turn, is randomly inserted into the genome of other strains of fruit flies. By chance, the GAL4 gene will sometimes land near regulatory DNA sequences that function only in certain nerve cells. If fruit fly strains containing these DNA sequences are crossed with another strain containing the gene for the light chain of the tetanus toxin, the resulting offspring will produce the active tetanus toxin inside certain nerve cells, which will disrupt the ability of those cells to communicate with adjacent muscles or nerves. That, in turn, helps determine the function of those specific nerve cells.

In one set of experiments using this system, designed to test the role of nerves in the development of vision, the tetanus toxin was expressed in all neurons associated with photoreceptors. As a consequence, the photoreceptors did not develop normally, and, not surprisingly, the flies were blind.[96]

In another example, designed to test the utility of *Drosophila* as a model for studying the effect of neural changes on cocaine addiction, tetanus toxin was expressed in nerves in the fly brain thought to be connected to some behavioral aspects of cocaine addiction. The expression of tetanus toxin in these nerves eliminated neurotransmitter release and prevented the stereotyped behaviors associated with cocaine addiction, supporting the use of *Drosophila* as a model for studying this phenomenon.[97]

USE OF TETANUS TOXIN TO TREAT PSYCHOLOGICAL CONDITIONS

There have been several reports indicating that tetanus toxin, or the heavy chain of tetanus toxin alone, can have a number of effects on nerve cells. For example, work by researchers in Spain showed that tetanus toxin prevents the re-uptake of serotonin. Since preventing the reuptake of serotonin is one mechanism for treating depression, nontoxic portions of tetanus toxin may have some potential for treating this condition.[98] In addition, the heavy chain of the tetanus toxin appears to offer some protection for neurons found in the brain. Brain cells growing in culture in the laboratory have been protected from death when the heavy chain of tetanus toxin was added.[99] Further research should help determine if the heavy chain of toxin may offer any therapeutic benefit in preserving nerve cells in people suffering from neurodegenerative disorders, like Parkinson disease.

TETANUS TOXIN AS A DELIVERY SYSTEM FOR TRANSPORTING PROTEINS TO THE CENTRAL NERVOUS SYSTEM

Tetanus toxin has the unusual ability to be specifically transported, via the peripheral nerves, to the central nervous system. This characteristic has been exploited in experiments designed to see if fragments of tetanus toxin can be used to transport therapeutic proteins to the spinal cord.

One important genetic disease involving the central nervous system is Tay-Sachs. It is caused by a mutation in an enzyme that normally breaks down **gangliosides**, components of cell membranes that contain carbohydrates and lipids. Because of this mutation, toxic concentrations of gangliosides accumulate in nerve cells and eventually kill critical nerve cells in the brain and spinal cord, typically resulting in death by age five. One strategy for treating the disease would be to try to replace the missing enzyme in the central nervous system. In experiments performed on nerve cells in culture, a combined protein, consisting of the heavy-chain fragment of tetanus toxin and the enzyme missing in Tay-Sachs patients, got into nerve cells and appeared to at least partially correct the genetic defect. Something like this might potentially work in a living person as well, although much additional work remains to be done before this might be considered for therapy.[100]

In another example, injury to the spine initiates a cascade of events that causes additional destruction of nervous tissue surrounding the damaged area by chemicals called oxygen radicals. One potential strategy to limit damage would be to treat the injured area with enzymes that destroy oxygen radicals. In one test of this hypothesis, superoxide dismutase, an enzyme that detoxifies oxygen radicals, was attached to the heavy chain fragment of tetanus toxin, which is involved in transport of the toxin to the central nervous system. When tested in neurons growing in culture in the laboratory, this hybrid protein appeared to be internalized and expressed in the cells,[101] suggesting that further tests would be warranted to determine whether this approach would have utility in living animals.

One concern about treatments using proteins fused to the heavy chain of tetanus toxin is that almost everyone in developed countries is vaccinated against tetanus, and the antibodies present in the blood might prevent the heavy chain from reaching the central nervous system. Fortunately, animal experiments performed by researchers from the U.S. Veterans Affairs Health Care System show that this is not likely to be a major stumbling block. These investigators injected the heavy chain of tetanus toxin into the animals and found equal amounts of it in the central nervous systems of animals that had been vaccinated with tetanus toxoid and in those that had not.[102] Therefore, using the nontoxic heavy chain of tetanus toxin may provide a useful strategy for treating central nervous system damage, although additional research will be required before this approach is tested in humans.

Considering the great potential for harm from *C. tetani* and tetanus toxin, it is intriguing that it may someday be possible to treat human ailments using this very potent poison. Continuing progress in understanding the biology of *C. tetani* may open additional options for treating disease or other damage to the central nervous system, based on the use of a fragment of the tetanus toxin.[103]

1. Lindley-Jones, M., D. Lewis, and J. Southgate. "Recurrent tetanus," *The Lancet* 363 (June 2004): 2048.

2. Centers for Disease Control. "Impact of Vaccines Universally Recommended for Children United States 1900–1998," *Morbidity and Mortality Weekly Report* 48 (April 1999): 243–248.

3. Byrd, T., and H.L. Ley. "*Clostridium tetani* in a Metropolitan area: Limited survey incorporating a simplified in Vitro Identification Test," *Applied Microbiology* 14, 2 (1966): 993–997.

4. Gilles, E. "Isolation of tetanus bacilli from street dust," *Journal of the American Medical Association* 109, 7 (1937): 484–486.

5. Tenbroeck, C, and J. Bauer. "The tetanus bacillus as an intestinal saprophyte in man," *Journal of Experimental Medicine* 36 (August 1922): 261–271.

6. Koransky, J.S. Allen, and V. Dowell. "Use of ethanol for selective isolation of sporeforming microorganisms," *Applied and Environmental Microbiology* 35 (1978): 762–765.

7. Cano, R., and M. Borucki. "Revival and Identification of Bacterial Spores in 25- to 40-Million-Year-Old Dominican Amber," *Science* 268 (May 1995): 1060–1064.

8. Dire, D. "Tetanus," E-Medicine.com. Available online. URL: http://www.emedicine.com/emerg/topic574.htm. Updated on December 1, 2005.

9. Bolton, B., and C. Fisch. "An estimate of the amount of toxin in the blood of horses infected with tetanus," *Transactions of the Association of American Physicians* 17 (1902): 462–467.

10. U.S. Food and Drug Administration. "The history of drug regulation in the United States: Biological therapeutics," FDA official Web site. Available online. URL: http://www.fda.gov/cder/centennial/history.htm#1902. Updated on May 26, 2006.

11. Beck, T., cited by Major. R.H. (ed). *Classic Descriptions of Disease.* Springfield, Ill.: Charles C. Thomas, 1945, 134.

12. Translation of the Edwin Smith Surgical Papyrus. Available online. URL: http://www.touregypt.net/edwin-smithsurgical.htm. Posted in 1996.

13. Scarborough, J. "Medicine." In: Grant, M., and R. Kitzinger (eds). *The Civilization of the Ancient Mediterranean*, vol. 2. New York: Charles Scribner's Sons, 1988, 1227–1228.

14. *The Extant Works of Aretaeus, the Cappadocian.* London: Sydenham Society, 1865, 253. Translated by Adams, F. Available online. Book 1, p. 8 of 253. URL: http://icarus.umkc.edu/sandbox/dh/aretaeusEnglish/page.7.a.php?size=240x320. Accessed November 5, 2007.

15. Veerasignam, P. "Analysis of the reported symptoms that preceded the death of King Rajasinghe of Sithawatke (1592 AD)," *Ceylon Medical Journal* 65, 2 (2002): 65–67.

16. Myerson, J. "More apropos of John Thoreau," *American Literature* 45 (1973): 104–106.

17. Woody, R., and E. Ross. "Neonatal Tetanus (St. Kilda, 19th Century)," *The Lancet* 1, 8650 (June 1989): 1339.

18. Carle, A., and G. Rattone. "Studio Esperimentale sull'eziologia del tetano," *Accademia di medicina di Torino Giornale della* 32 (1884): 174–179.

19. Nicolaier, A. "Uber infectiosen Tetanus," *Deutsche medizinische Wocheschrift* 10 (1884): 842–844.

20. Kitasato, S. "Uber den Tetanusbacillus," *Zeitschrift fur Hygiene* 7 (1890): 224–234; Bartholomew, J. "Japanese Nobel Candidates in the First Half of the Twentieth Century," *Osiris, 2d Series* 13 (1998): 238–284.

21. Pitzurra, M. "The History of Tetanus," in *Eighth International Conference on Tetanus.* Nistico, G., B. Bizzini, B. Bytchenko, and R. Triau (eds). Rome-Milan, Italy: Pythagora Press, 1989, 1–15.

22. Behring, E., and S. Kitasato. "The mechanism of immunity in animals

Endnotes

to diphtheria and tetanus," *Deutsche Medizinishe Wochenschrift* 16 (1890): 1113–1114.

23. Nocard, E. "Sur la serotherapie du tetanos. Essais de traitement preventif," *Bulletin de l'Academie de medecine* 37 (1895): 407–418.

24. Wilson, E. "Neurosurgical treatment for tetanus," *Journal of the History of the Neurosciences* 6, 1 (1997): 82–85.

25. Nobel Foundation. "Biography of Paul Ehrlich," Nobel Foundation Online. Available online. URL: http://nobelprize.org/nobel_prizes/medicine/laureates/1908/ehrlich-bio.html. Downloaded on March 14, 2007.

26. Lowenstein, E. "Ti Uber immunisierung mit toxoiden des tetanustoxin," *Zeitschrift fur Hygiene* 62 (1909): 491–494.

27. Eisler, M. "Uber Immunisierung mit durch Formaldehyde veranderten Tetansutoxinen," *Wiener Klinische Wochenschrift* 45 (1915): 1223–1225.

28. Vallee H., and Bazy L. "Sur la vaccination active de l'homme contre le tetanos," *Comptes rendus hebomadaires des seances de l'Academie des sciences* 164 (1917): 1019–1022.

29. Descombey, P. "L' anatoxine tetanique," *Comptes rendus hebdomadaires des seances et memoires de la Societe de Biologie* 91 (1924): 233–234.

30. Ramon, G., and P. Descombey. "Sur l'immunisation antitetanique et sur la production de l'antitoxine tetanique," *Comptes rendus hebdomadaires des seances et memoires de la Societe de Biologie* 93 (1925): 711.

31. Ramon, G., and C. Zoller. "De la valeur antigenique de l'anatoxine tetanique chez l'homme," *Comptes rendus hebomadaires des seances de l'Academie des sciences* 182 (1926): 245–247.

32. Gold, H. Untitled letter. *Journal of the American Medical Association* 109, 7 (August 1937): 484.

33. Tillman, D. "Tetanus," *The Western Journal of Medicine* 129, 2 (1978): 107–109.

34. Sanford, J. "Tetanus—forgotten but not gone," *The New England Journal of Medicine* 332, 12 (1995): 812–813.

35. Centers for Disease Control. "Tetanus. Pink Book," CDC official Web site. Available online. URL: http://www.cdc.gov/vaccines/pubs/pinkbook/downloads/tetanus.pdf. Downloaded on February 1, 2007; Wikipedia. "Orders of magnitude (mass)." Available online. URL: http://en.wikipedia.org/wiki/1_E-25_kg. Downloaded on February 17, 2007.

36. Middlebrook, J. "Cell Surface Receptors for Protein Toxins," in *Botulinum neurotoxin and Tetanus Toxin*. Simpson, L. (ed). San Diego, Calif.: Academic Press, 1989.

37. Chen, F., G. Kuziemko, and R. Stevens. "Biophysical Characterization of the Stability of the 150-Kilodalton Botulinum Toxin, the Nontoxic Component, and the 900-Kilodalton Botulinum Toxin Complex Species," *Infection and Immunity* 66, 6 (June 1998): 2420–2425.

38. Raffestin, S., J. Marvaud, R. Cerrato, B. Dupuy, and M. Popoff. "Organization and regulation of the neurotoxin genes in *Clostridium botulinum* and *Clostridium tetani*," *Anaerobe* 10 (2004): 93–100.

39. Schiavo, G., O. Rossetto, F. Tonello, and C. Montecucco. "Intracellular targets and metalloprotease activity of tetanus and botulism neurotoxins," in *Clostridial Neurotoxins*. New York: Springer, 1995.

40. Lalli, G., S. Bohnert, K. Deinhardt, C. Verastegui, and G. Schivao. "The journey of tetanus and botulinum neurotoxins in neurons," *Trends in Microbiology* 11, 9 (2003): 431–437.

41. Grumelli, C., C. Verderio, D. Pozzi, O. Rossetto, C. Montecucco, and M. Mateoli. "Internalization and mechanism of action of clostridial toxins in neurons," *Neurotoxicology* 26 (2005): 761–767.

42. Warbasse, J. "Immunity Against Tetanus," *Annals of Surgery* 19, 6 (June 1894): 699–704.
43. Duchen, L., and D. Tonge. "The effects of tetanus toxin on neuromuscular transmission and on the morphology of motor end-plates in slow and fast skeletal muscle of the mouse," *Journal of Physiology* 228 (1973): 157–172.
44. Shelton, D., and R. Penciner. "Case report of an unusual source of tetanus," *Journal of Emergency Medicine* 16, 2 (1998): 163–165.
45. Bleck, T. "*Clostridium tetani,*" in *Principles and Practices of Infectious Disease.* Mandell, G., D. Gordon, and J. Bennett (eds). New York: Churchill Livingstone, Inc., 1995.
46. Flowers, M., and R. Edmondson. "Long-term recovery from tetanus: a study of 50 survivors," *British Medical Journal* 280, 6210 (1980): 303–305.
47. *The Extant Works of Aretaeus, the Cappadocian.* Translated by F. Adams. London: Sydenham Society, 1865, 253.
48. Dennis, F. "The treatment of tetanus," *Annals of Surgery* 26, 6 (December 1897): 657–665.
49. Milledge, J. "Hyperbaric oxygen therapy in tetanus," *Journal of the American Medical Association* 203, 10 (1968): 155–156.
50. Barry, Dave. "Medical Boom," *Miami Herald.* January 21, 1996.
51. Goode, B., K. Caruso, J. Murphy, A. Weber, and J. Burgett. "Neonatal Tetanus—Montana, 1998." *Morbidity and Mortality Weekly Report* 47, 43 (November 6, 1998): 928–930.
52. Thaysen-Andersen, M., S. Jørgensen, E. Wilhelmsen, J. Petersen, and P. Højrup. "Investigation of the detoxification mechanism of formaldehyde-treated tetanus toxin," *Vaccine* 25 (2007): 2213–2227.
53. Ehreth, J. "The global value of vaccination," *Vaccine* 21 (2003): 596–600.
54. Lloyd, J., P. Haber, G. Mootrey, M. Braun, P. Rhodes, R. Chen, VAERS Working Group. "Adverse event reporting rates following tetanus-diphtheria and tetanus toxoid vaccinations: data from the Vaccine Adverse Event Reporting System (VAERS), 1991–1997," *Vaccine* 21 (2003): 3746–3750.
55. Rosenthal S., and R.T. Chen. "The reporting sensitivities of two passive surveillance systems for vaccine adverse events," *American Journal of Public Health* 85, 12 (1995): 1706–1709.
56. Czeizel, A., and M. Rockenbauer. "Tetanus toxoid and congenital abnormalities," *International Journal of Gynecology and Obstetrics* 64 (1999): 253–258.
57. U.S. Health and Human Services Department. Health Resources and Services Administration. "Vaccine injury compensation table." Available online. URL: http://www.hrsa. gov/vaccinecompensation/table.htm. Downloaded on February 1, 2007.
58. Bohlke, K., R. Davis, S. Marcy, M. Braun, F. DeStefano, S. Black, J. Mullooly, and R. Thompson for the Vaccine Safety Datalink Team. "Risk of Anaphylaxis After Vaccination of Children and Adolescents," *Pediatrics* 112 (2003): 815–820.
59. Braun, M., G. Mootrey, M. Salive, R. Chen, S. Ellenberg, and the VAERS Working Group. "Infant immunization with acellular pertussis vaccines in the US: Assessment of the first two years' data from the Vaccine Adverse Event Reporting System (VAERS)," *Pediatrics* 106 (2000): e51.
60. Dillin, L., F. Hoaglund, and M. Scheck. "Brachial neuritis," *The Journal of Bone and Joint Surgery* 7 (1985): 878–880.
61. Ulanova, M., A. Tarkowski, M. Hahn-Zoric, and L. Hanson. "The Common Vaccine Adjuvant Aluminum Hydroxide Up-Regulates Accessory Properties of Human Monocytes via an Interleukin-4-Dependent Mechanism," *Infection and Immunity* 69, 2 (February 2001): 1151–1159.

Endnotes

62. Fair, E., T. Murphy, A. Golaz, and M. Wharton. "Philosophic objection to vaccination as a risk for tetanus among children younger than 15 years," *Pediatrics* 109, 1 (2002): 1–3.

63. Matzkin, H., and S. Regev. "Naturally acquired immunity to tetanus toxin in an isolated community," *Infection and Immunity* 48, 1 (1985): 267–268.

64. Veronesi, R., B. Bizzini, R. Focaccia, A. Coscina, C. Mazza, M. Focaccia, F. Carraro, and M. Honingman. "Naturally acquired antibodies to tetanus toxin in humans and animals from the Galapagos Islands," *The Journal of Infectious Diseases* 147, 2 (1983): 308–311.

65. Veronesi, R., H. Cecin, A. Correa, J. Tavares, C. Morales, and O.J. Bertoldo. "New concepts on tetanus immunization: naturally acquired immunity," *Journal of Hygiene, Epidemiology, Microbiology, and Epidemiology* 19 (1975): 126–134.

66. Abrahamian, F., C. Pollack, F. LoVecchio, R. Nanda, and R. Carlson. "Fatal Tetanus in a drug abuser with protective antitetanus antibodies," *The Journal of Emergency Medicine* 18, 2 (2000): 189–193.

67. Beeching, N., and N. Crowcroft. "Tetanus in injecting drug users," *British Medical Journal* 330 (2005): 208–209.

68. Pascual, F., E. McGinlye, L. Zanarid, M. Cortese, and T. Murphy. "Tetanus Surveillance—United States 1998–2000," *Morbidity and Mortality Weekly Report* 55, SS03 (2003): 1–8.

69. Hahne, S., J. White, N. Crowcroft, M. Brett, R. George, N. Beeching, K. Roy, and D. Goldberg. "Tetanus in injection drug users, United Kingdom," *Emerging Infectious Diseases* 12, 4 (2006): 709–710.

70. Atabek, M., and O. Pirgon. "Tetanus in a fully-immunized child," *The Journal of Emergency Medicine* 29, 3 (2005): 345–346.

71. Vinson, D. "Tetanus not 100% preventable," *Journal of Emergency Medicine* 17, 4 (1999): 745–747.

72. Pryor, T., C. Onarecker, and T. Coniglione. "Elevated antitoxin titers in a man with generalized tetanus," *The Journal of Family Practice* 44 (1997): 299–303.

73. McQuillan, G., D. Kruszon-Moran, A. Defores, S. Chu, and M. Wharton. "Serologic immunity to diphtheria and tetanus in the United States," *Annals of Internal Medicine* 136, 9 (2002): 660–666.

74. Dire, D. "Tetanus," E-Medicine.com. Available online. URL: http://www.emedicine.com/emerg/topic574.htm. Updated on December 1, 2005.

75. Jojosky, R., and others. "Summary of notifiable diseases, 2004," *Morbidity and Mortality Weekly Report* 53 (2006): 1–79.

76. S. Kruger, M. Seyfarth, K. Sacka, and B. Kreft. "Defective immune response to tetanus toxoid in hemodialysis patients and its association with diphtheria vaccination" *Vaccine* 17 (1999): 1145–1150.

77. Opravil, M., W. Fierz, L. Matter, J. Blaser, and R. Luthy. "Poor antibody response after tetanus and pneumococcal vaccination in immunocompromised, HIV-infected patients," *Clinical and Experimental Immunology* 2 (May 1991): 185–9; and Kroon, F.P., J. van Dissel, J. de Jong, and R. van Furth. "Antibody response to influenza, tetanus and pneumococcal vaccines in HIV-seropositive individuals in relation to the number of CD4+ lymphocytes," *AIDS* 4 (April 1994): 469–476.

78. Fair, E., T. Murphy, A. Golaz, and M. Wharton. "Philosophic objection to vaccination as a risk for tetanus among children younger than 15 years," *Pediatrics* 109, 1 (2002): E2.

79. Hanley, M., W. O'Regan, S. Squires, and C. Tate. "Tetanus, pneumonia, and malaria in a tsunami victim in Banda

Aceh, Indonesia," *Military Medicine* 171, 12 (December 2006): 1187–1189.

80. Bennett, J., C. Ma, H. Traverso, S. B. Agha, and J. Boring. "Neonatal tetanus associated with topical umbilical ghee: covert role of cow dung," *International Journal of Epidemiology* 28 (1999): 1172–1175.

81. Centers for Disease Control. "Tetanus. Pink Book," CDC official Web site. Available online. URL: http://www.cdc. gov/vaccines/pubs/pinkbook/down-loads/tetanus.pdf. Downloaded on February 1, 2007; Wikipedia. "Orders of magnitude (mass)." Available online. URL: http://en.wikipedia.org/wiki/1_ E-25_kg. Downloaded on February 17, 2007.

82. Ehreth, J. "The global value of vaccination," *Vaccine* 21 (2003): 596–600.

83. Vandelaer, J., M. Birmingham, F. Gasse, M. Kurian, C. Shaw, and S. Garnier. "Tetanus in developing countries: an update on the maternal and neonatal tetanus elimination initiative," *Vaccine* 21 (2003): 3442–3445.

84. Centers for Disease Control. "Vaccine Preventable Deaths and the Global Immunization Vision and Strategy, 2006–2015," *Morbidity and Mortality Weekly Report* 55, 18 (2006): 511–515.

85. Habib, A. "Tetanus complicating snakebite in northern Nigeria: clinical presentation and public health implications," *Acta Tropica* 85 (2003): 87–91.

86. Jaganathan, K.Y. Rao, P. Singh, D. Prabakaran, S. Gupta, A. Jain, and S. Vyas. "Development of a single dose tetanus toxoid formulation based on polymeric microspheres: a comparative student of poly(D, L-lactic-co-glycolic acid) versus chitosan microspheres," *International Journal of Pharmaceutics* 294 (2005): 23–32.

87. Medaglini, D., A. Ciabattini, M. Spinosa, T. Maggi, H. Marcotte, M. Oggioni, and G. Pozzi. "Immunization with recombinant *Streptococcus gordonii* expressing tetanus toxin fragment C confers protection from lethal challenge in mice," *Vaccine* 19, 15–16 (February 2001): 1931–1939.

88. Martin, L., F. Cornille, S. Furcaud, H. Meudal, B. Roques, and M. Fournie-Zaluski. "Metallopeptidase inhibitors of tetanus toxin: A combinatorial approach," *Journal of Medicinal Chemistry* 42 (1999): 515–525.

89. Bruggemann, H., et al. "The genome sequence of *Clostridium tetani*, the causative agent of tetanus disease," *Proceedings of the National Academy of Sciences, USA* 100, 3 (2003): 1316–1321.

90. Bruggemann, H., and G. Gottschalk. "Insights in metabolism and toxin production from the complete genome sequence of *Clostridium tetani*," *Anaerobe* 10 (2004): 53–68.

91. Raffestin, S., J. Marvaud, R. Cerrato, B. Dupuy, and M. Popoff. "Organization and regulation of the neurotoxin genes in *Clostridium botulinum* and *Clostridium tetani*," *Anaerobe* 10 (2004): 93–100.

92. Lyras, D., and J. Rood. "Clostridial Genetics," in *Gram-Positive Pathogens*, 2d ed. V. Fischetti et al. Washington, D.C.: ASM Press, 2006, 672–687.

93. Thwaites, C. "Tetanus," *Current Anaesthesia & Critical Care* 16, 1 (February 2005): 50–57; and Thwaites, C., and J. Farrar. "Preventing and treating tetanus," *British Medical Journal* 326 (2003): 117–118.

94. Thwaites, C., I. Yen, H. Loan, T. Thuy, G. Thwaites, K. Stepniewska, N. Soni, N. White, and N. Farrar. "Magnesium sulphate for treatment of severe tetanus: a randomised controlled trial," *Lancet* 368 (2006): 1436–1443.

95. Grumelli, C., C. Verderio, D. Pozzi, O. Rossetto, C. Montecucco, and M. Mateoli. "Internalization and mechanism of action of clostridial toxins in neurons," *Neurotoxicology* 26 (2005): 761–767.

96. Martin, J.R., A. Keller, and S. Sweeney. "Targeted expression of tetanus toxin: A new tool to study the neurobiology

Endnotes

of behavior," *Advances in Genetics* 47 (2002): 1–47.

97. Martin, J.R., A. Keller, and S. Sweeney. "Targeted expression of tetanus toxin: A new tool to study the neurobiology of behavior," *Advances in Genetics* 47 (2002): 1–47.

98. Gil, C., A. Najib, and J. Aguilera. "Serotonin transport is modulated differently by tetanus toxin and growth factors," *Neurochemistry International* 42 (2003): 535–542; and Inserte, J., A. Najib, P. Pelliccioni, C. Gil, and J. Aguilera. "Inhibition by Tetanus Toxin of Sodium-Dependent, High-Affinity [3H]5-Hydroxytryptamine Uptake in Rat Synaptosomes," *Biochemical Pharmacology* 57 (1999): 111–120.

99. Chaib-Oukadour, I., C. Gil, and J. Aguilera. "The C-terminal domain of the heavy chain of tetanus toxin rescues cerebellar granule neurones from apoptotic death: involvement of phosphatidylinositol 3-kinase and mitogen-activated protein kinase pathways," *Journal of Neurochemistry* 90, 5 (September 2004): 1227–36.

100. Dobrens, K., A. Joseph, and M. Rattazzi. "Neuronal lysosomal enzyme replacement using fragment C of tetanus toxin," *Proceedings of the National Academy of Sciences* 89 (1992): 2297–2301.

101. Francis, J., B. Hosler, R. Brown, and P. Fishman. "CuZn Superoxide dismutase (SOD-1): Tetanus Toxin Fragment C Hybrid Protein for Targeted Delivery of SOD-1 for Neuronal Cells," *The Journal of Biological Chemistry* 270 (1995): 15, 434–15, 424.

102. Fishman, P.S., C. Matthews, D. Parks, M. Box, and N. Fairweather. "Immunization does not interfere with uptake and transport by motor neurons of the binding fragment of tetanus toxin," *Journal of Neuroscience Research* 83, 8 (June 2006): 1540–1543.

103. Rossetto, O., M. Seveso, P. Caccin, G. Schiavo, and C. Montecucco. "Tetanus and botulinum neurotoxins: turning bad guys into good by research," *Toxicon* 39 (2001) 27–41.

adjuvant—A chemical included in a vaccine that enhances the ability of the vaccine to immunize against a disease.

anaerobic—Without oxygen. *C. tetani* requires anaerobic conditions for growth.

antibodies—Proteins, produced by immune system cells, that have the ability to inactivate toxins or attack bacterial pathogens.

antitoxin—Serum containing antibodies that can neutralize the tetanus toxin.

ATP—Adenosine Tri-Phosphate. The primary energy storage molecule in cells. *C. tetani* uses an unusual process of pumping sodium atoms across the cell membrane to produce ATP.

autonomic nervous system—The part of the nervous system that is not under conscious control. In late-stage tetanus, some patients die when the autonomic nervous system is affected by tetanus toxin and the heart no longer functions properly.

centrifuge—A machine that spins tubes at a high speed. The force of the spinning causes cells or small particles to form a pellet at the bottom of a tube.

cephalic tetanus—Tetanus that is initially confined to the head, normally the result of a *C. tetani*-infected wound in that part of the body.

Clostridium tetani—The bacterium that causes tetanus.

dalton—A measure of the size of a molecule. One dalton corresponds to the weight of one hydrogen atom.

electroporation—A technique for introducing foreign DNA into a cell. Electroporation involves mixing the bacteria with DNA, followed by exposure to a high voltage pulse. This transiently puts holes into the bacterial cell membrane and allows DNA to enter the cell.

enzyme—A protein that catalyzes a specific chemical reaction. As a catalyst, an enzyme assists in allowing a chemical reaction to occur without being used up during the reaction.

formaldehyde—A chemical disinfectant, which is used to make tetanus toxoid for vaccinations.

formalin—A solution of 37 percent formaldehyde in water.

gangliosides—Components of cell membranes that contain carbohydrates and lipids.

Glossary

generalized tetanus—Tetanus that affects the entire body, the result of tetanus toxin affecting the central nervous system.

genome—The entire set of genetic instructions encoded in the DNA of an organism.

immunized—Made immune. For example, a person given a series of tetanus vaccinations will be immunized against tetanus.

immunoglobulins—See ANTIBODIES.

inhibitory neuron—A nerve cell located in the spinal column, which signals muscles to stop contraction. This type of nerve is specifically targeted by the tetanus toxin.

localized tetanus—Muscle contraction caused by tetanus that is confined to a small region of the body. Can sometimes develop into generalized tetanus.

messenger RNA (mRNA)—A form of ribonucleic acid that acts as an intermediary between the DNA and the protein encoded by the DNA. Messenger RNA is made by RNA polymerase and is translated into protein by the ribosome.

metalloproteases—Enzymes that cut other proteins; they require metals, such as zinc, for activity.

microspheres—Microscopic beads. When used for vaccination the antigen, like tetanus toxoid, is embedded in the tiny beads. The beads then break down slowly in the body, potentially prolonging the immune response, and leading to a stronger effect from vaccination.

motor neuron—A nerve involved in activating muscle movement.

neonatal tetanus—Tetanus that develops in infants following birth, normally from a *C. tetani* infection of the umbilical cord.

neurotransmitters—Molecules released from nerves that activate or inhibit adjacent nerve cells.

obligate anaerobe—An organism (like *C. tetani*) that can grow only in the absence of oxygen.

opisthotonos—Severe muscle contractions in tetanus that lead to a characteristic arching of the back.

pathogen—A disease-causing microbe.

plasmid—A small circular DNA. Plasmids often carry virulence factors or toxin genes. In *C. tetani*, the tetanus toxin gene is found on a plasmid.

protease—An enzyme that breaks down proteins.

retrograde transport—A system that moves materials from neurons at the periphery of the body to the spinal cord.

risus sardonicus—A symptom of tetanus that literally means a "sardonic smile"; as a result of muscle contractions of the facial muscles, a person with the disease often appears to have a sarcastic smile.

sensor proteins—Proteins usually located on the cell surface that recognize, and trigger a response to, an environmental signal.

sigma factor—A component of RNA polymerase that recognizes sites on the DNA in order to start transcription.

SNARE proteins—These are *S*oluble *NSF* *A*ccessory protein *R*eceptors; they play a role in transporting other proteins out of a cell. Tetanus toxin specifically inactivates one of these proteins, called synaptobrevin or VAMP, in nerve cells. As a consequence, the nerve cell cannot send out inhibitory signals to other neurons.

spores—An inert stage of an organism. Some bacteria, like *C. tetani*, produce spores that can survive for decades in the environment.

strychnine—A poison that produces some symptoms similar to tetanus.

synaptic vesicles—Compartments in nerve cells, surrounded by a lipid membrane, which contain neurotransmitters. Tetanus toxin enters nerve cells by moving into synaptic vesicles. The toxin also prevents synaptic vesicles from fusing with the nerve cell membrane and releasing neurotransmitters.

synaptobrevin—Also called VAMP, for vesicle-associated membrane protein. A SNARE protein in nerve cells that is required for transmission of signals from one nerve to an adjacent nerve. This protein is specifically cleaved by tetanus toxin.

tetanospasmin—A toxin, produced by the bacterium *C. tetani*, which causes the strong muscle contractions that are the primary symptoms of the disease.

tetanus—A disease, caused by *C. tetani*, resulting from the tetanus toxin tetanospasmin. The key symptom of tetanus is uncontrolled muscle contraction; often the first symptom is lockjaw, caused by contractions of the masseter muscles.

tetanus immunoglobulin—Antibodies that bind to tetanus toxin (tetanospasmin) and inactivate it.

Glossary

toxin—A natural chemical that is lethal in very small doses. Tetanospasmin is one of the most potent toxins known.

toxoid—An inactivated form of a toxin. For example, tetanus toxin in the current vaccine is inactivated by treatment with formaldehyde and lysine to create tetanus toxoid.

transcription—In the cell, the process of converting DNA to RNA using the enzyme RNA polymerase.

transposon—A section of DNA that is capable of moving from one part of a DNA molecule to another, or into a new DNA molecule. Transposons are used by geneticists to mutate genes; when the transposon inserts into a new DNA molecule it often inactivates the gene where it inserts.

trismus—Contraction of muscles required for chewing—also called *lockjaw*. This is frequently one of the first symptoms of tetanus.

upstream activating sequence (UAS)—Upstream activating sequences are DNA sequences that, in the presence of the appropriate signals, activate transcription of an adjacent gene. In one system designed to study the function of specific cells or tissues, a UAS has been genetically engineered to selectively activate tetanus toxin in certain cells in animals.

virulence factors—Attributes of pathogens that allow them to circumvent the immune system and cause disease.

Further Resources

Web Sites

Mayo Clinic: Tetanus
   http://www.mayoclinic.com/health/tetanus/DS00227

MedlinePlus: Tetanus
   http://www.nlm.nih.gov/medlineplus/ency/article/000615.htm

National Center for Infectious Disease, Centers for Disease Control: Infectious Disease Information: Tetanus (Lockjaw, *Clostridium tetani* Infection)
   http://www.cdc.gov/ncidod/diseases/submenus/sub_tetanus.htm

World Health Organization: Tetanus
   http://www.who.int/topics/tetanus/en/

Index

adjuvant, 33, 61, 89
allergies, to vaccine, 29, 50, 60
alum, 61
amino-acid degrading enzymes, 76
Amish, 68
anaerobic (defined), 89
anaerobic tissue, 50
anaphylaxis, 60
animals, as tetanus hosts, 18–19
animal testing, of vaccine, 26–29
antibiotics, 40, 50
antibodies
  defined, 89
  in dialysis patients, 67
  ineffective, 65
  and prevention of neonatal tetanus, 14
  for testing of vaccine potency, 32
  in unvaccinated individuals, 62–63
  in vaccinated individuals, 65–66
  and vaccine production, 29
  and vaccine testing on humans, 33–34
antitoxin, 89. *See also* tetanus immunoglobulin
anxiety, as effect of tetanus, 51
Aretaeus, the Cappadocian, 21, 52
ATP (adenosine triphosphate), 76, 89
autonomic nervous system, 77, 89

back. *See* opisthotonos
Bauer, J., 11
Bazy, L., 30–31
Behring, Emil, 26–27
Biologics Control Act (1902), 19

black widow spider bites, 17
bleeding, as early treatment, 52
blood, 27
booster shots, 57, 67
Bordetella pertussis, 57
*bot*R gene, 75
botulinum, tetanus vs., 42–43, 72
botulinum toxin, 40
botulism, 42
brachial neuritis, 60
brain, injection of tetanus immunoglobulin into, 28
Brazil, 63
breathing, tetanus treatment and, 50
butter (on umbilical cord), 70

carbolic acid, 52
cardiac arrest, 77
Carle, Antonio, 22
cautery, 52
celebrities, tetanus deaths of, 21–22
cell membrane, 76
cellular biology, 78–80
Centers for Disease Control and Prevention, 68
central nervous system
  infections of, 17
  tetanus toxin as protein delivery system to, 81–83
centrifuge, 31, 89
cephalic tetanus, 16, 89
characteristics, of tetanus, 12–16
children. *See also* neonatal tetanus
  immunization schedule, 58
  tainted diphtherium serum case, 18
  vaccination of, 68

chromosome, and virulence factors, 74–75
Civil War, 22
Clostridium acetobutylium, 75
Clostridium botulinum, 40, 75
Clostridium perfringens, 75
Clostridium tetani
  as anaerobic bacterium, 12, 25
  as cause of tetanus, 10, 38–47
  defined, 89
  and disease presentation, 16
  entry into body, 12
  in environment, 10–11
  first isolation of bacterium, 24–25
  growth in human body, 38–40
  in heroin users, 65
  identification of, 22–26
  insights from genome sequencing, 73–76
  metabolism of, 75–76
  nutrients for, 26, 39–40, 76
  potency of toxin, 15
  virulence factors, 74–75
cocaine addiction, 80
collagenase, 39–40, 74
colonization, of wound sites, 39
*col*T gene, 74
complex, of proteins, 42–43
Congress, U.S., 19
contamination, of vaccine, 18–19, 32
controlled studies, 77
cross-linking, of proteins, 56–57
curare, 52
cytoplasm, 47, 76

dalton, 43, 44, 89
death rate. *See* mortality
   rate
Dennis, F., 52–53
depression treatment,
   80–81
Descombey, P., 33, 54
detoxification, of tetanus
   toxin, 29–30
developing countries
   neonatal tetanus in, 16
   new approaches to treat-
     ment in, 77–78
   status of tetanus in,
     70–71
dialysis patients, 66–67
digestive enzymes, 42–43
diphtheria
   and DPT shot, 34, 57
   immunoglobulin treat-
     ments for, 29
   vaccination to prevent
     epidemics, 60
diphtheria antitoxin, 18
disease management, 77–78
DNA sequencing, of *C. tetani* genome, 73–76
dogs, 18, 23
Drosophila melanogaster,
   78–80
drugs, contamination by
   tetanus toxin, 18–19
drug users, tetanus risk for,
   64–65
DTaP vaccine, 57
DTP vaccine, 34, 70–71
dung, as source of spores,
   70

ear canal, cephalic tetanus
   and, 16
Edwin Smith Surgical
   Papyrus, 20
Ehrlich, Paul, 28–29
Eisler, Michael, 30, 32, 54
elderly tetanus victims,
   66, 67

electroporation, 77, 89
encapsulation, of tetanus
   toxoid, 72–73
Enterococcus faecalis, 76
environment, *C. tetani* in,
   10–11
enzyme
   and *C. tetani* nutrition,
     39–40
   defined, 89
   lipid-degrading, 76
   metalloproteases, 75
   and tetanus toxin activa-
     tion, 44
epidemics, 60
"Epidemics" (Hippocrates),
   20–21
Ethiopia, 62–63
ethyl alcohol, 12

Faber, Knud, 26
facial paralysis, cephalic
   tetanus and, 16
food, botulism and, 42–43
Food and Drug
   Administration, U.S.,
   19
formaldehyde
   defined, 89
   for prevention of vaccine
     contamination, 32
   for toxin inactivation, 29,
     30, 33, 56
formalin, 32, 89
frogs, 18, 47
fructose, 76
fruit flies, 79
fulmar, 23
future issues, 72–82

Galapagos Islands, 63
GAL4 protein, 79–80
gangliosides, 81, 89
gastrointestinal tract,
   42–43, 63
geese, susceptibility to tetanus, 18

gene
   for encoding tetanus
     toxin, 40, 73, 78–80
   for encoding virulence
     factor, 41
generalized tetanus, 16, 90
genetic engineering, 73,
   76–77, 79
genetic studies, 76–77
genome, 40, 41, 90
genome sequencing, of *C.
tetani,* 73–76
Germany, 66–67
ghee, 70
Global Immunization
   Vision and Strategy, 71
glucose, for *C. tetani*
   growth, 75
goats, susceptibility to tetanus, 18
Gold, Herman, 34–35
guinea pigs
   susceptibility to tetanus,
     18
   tetanus bacterium experi-
     ments, 23
   tetanus immunoglobulin
     experiments, 28
   vaccine testing experi-
     ments, 30, 33

head wound, cephalic tetanus and, 16
heart, 16, 50–51
heat
   for *C. tetani* spore isola-
     tion, 24, 25
   for vaccine preparation, 33
heat resistance, of *C. tetani*
   spores, 24
heavy chain
   toxin activation, 44
heavy chain, of botulism
   toxin, 42
heavy chain, of tetanus
   toxin
   binding to synapse, 44

Index

formaldehyde's effect on, 57
neuron protection by, 81
and spine injury treatment, 82
and Tay-Sachs treatment, 81
and tetanus toxin transport, 44–47
hemolysin, 75
heroin users, 64, 65
Hippocrates, 20–21, 52
historical figures, tetanus deaths of, 21–22
historical treatments for tetanus, 52–54
history, of tetanus, 20–37
HIV (human immunodeficiency virus), 67
horses
  susceptibility to tetanus, 18
  tetanus immunoglobulin production by, 29, 31–32, 50
  vaccine testing on, 30, 33
hosts, animal, 18–19
human immunoglobulin, 29
human vaccine tests, 30, 33–34
hydrochloric acid, 52
hyperbaric chamber, 54

illicit drug use. See injection drug users, tetanus risk for
immune response
  and adjuvants, 61
  and inactive toxin, 29–30
  and side effects, 58
  and tetanus toxin production, 40
immune system
  circumventing by C. tetani, 15
  of elderly individuals, 66
  need for oxygen by, 39

immunity, natural, 62–63
immunization. See vaccination
immunized (defined), 90
immunocompromised individuals, 66–68
immunoglobulins, 28–29, 90. See also tetanus immunoglobulin
inactivated toxin, 29–30
incubation period, 12–14
Indian Ocean tsunami (2004), 68–69
infants. See neonatal tetanus
inhibitory neuron
  defined, 90
  effect of tetanus toxin on, 13, 46
  and light chain, 47
  and retrograde transport, 46–47
inhibitory signals, 47
injection drug users, tetanus risk for, 64–65
injuries. See wounds
intensive care, 49, 51, 53
intravenous feeding, 50
invertebrates, susceptibility to tetanus by, 18
iodine, 30
ion channel, 47
iron, for C. tetani nutrition, 39
isolation, of tetanus bacterium, 24–25

kidney dialysis patients, 66–67
Kitasato, Shibasburo, 24–27
Koch, Robert, 24

light, for toxin inactivation, 29–30
light chain, of botulism toxin, 42

light chain, of tetanus toxin
  in Drosophila melanogaster, 78–80
  in inhibitory neuron, 47
  and toxin activation, 44
  and toxin inactivation, 57
  and toxin transport, 47
lipid-degrading enzymes, 76
lipids, for C. tetani nutrition, 76
localized tetanus, 16, 90
lockjaw, 14
Lowenstein, Ernst, 29–30, 54
lysine, 56, 57

magnesium sulfate, 78
mammals, susceptibility to tetanus by, 18
management, of disease, 77–78
mechanism of tetanus disease, 38–47
messenger RNA (mRNA), 41, 90
metabolism, of C. tetani, 75–76
metalloproteases, 75, 90
metronidazole, 50
mice
  immune response after vaccination, 73
  susceptibility to tetanus, 18
  tetanus from pure bacteria cultures, 26
  tetanus from soil particle injection, 23
  and tetanus immunoglobulin, 27
microspheres, 72, 90
middle ear infection, cephalic tetanus and, 16
monkeys, 18
Montagu, George, 21
Monvoisin, A., 32

mortality rate
  in developing countries,
    70–71
  U.S. (1900-2000), 69
  U.S. (1940s), 10, 49, 69
  U.S. (current), 50, 70
  from vaccination, 59
motor neuron, 13, 90
multiple vaccinations, 34
muscle contractions
  botulinum vs. tetanus
    toxin, 72
  as characteristic of teta-
    nus, 10
  and inhibitory neurons,
    13
  and retrograde transport,
    47
  from toxin's action on
    nerve cells, 47
muscle spasms, 14, 16
mutation, and genetic
  manipulation, 76–77

National Vaccine Injury
  Compensation
  Program, 60
natural disasters, tetanus
  following, 68–69
natural immunity, 62–63
neonatal tetanus
  defined, 16, 90
  in developing countries,
    70
  Montana case, 55
  St. Kilda, Scotland
    depopulation, 23
nerve cells
  and toxin, 18, 44, 45
  and treatment, 48
nerve-muscle junction. See
  synapse
nerves
  action of tetanus toxin
    on, 47, 78–80
  treatment to interfere
    with toxin action, 73

neurodegenerative disor-
  ders, 81
neurons, protection of, 81
neurotransmitters, 13, 90
neutralization, of tetanus
  toxin, 50
Nicolaier, Arthur, 23–24, 26
Nigeria, 71
Nocard, Edmond, 28
nutrients, for C. tetani, 26,
  38–40, 76

obligate anaerobe, 15, 38, 90
opisthotonos, 20, 90
oxygen
  as C. tetani growth inhib-
    itor, 12, 25, 38
  and immune system, 39
oxygen radicals, 82

pacemaker, 51
Pakistan, 70
Pasteur, Louis, 22–23
Pasteur Institute, 31
pathogen, 11, 90
penicillin, 50
Peninsular War, 36, 37
peripheral nerves, 81
pertussis, DPT shot for, 34
pH, 47
photoreceptors, 80
pigeons, 18
plasmid, 41, 74, 90
potassium iodide, 30
potency, of C. tetani toxin,
  15
Powell, Joe, 22
pregnancy, vaccination
  during, 59
presentations, of tetanus
  disease, 16
pressure chamber, 53
prevention, 55–63
protease, 40, 91
protein
  and cell communica-
    tion, 78

as C. tetani nutrient, 26,
  38–39
and immune response, 61
nerve cell. See synapto-
  brevin
SNARE, 78, 91
tetanus toxin as delivery
  system of, 81–83
in tetanus toxoid vac-
  cine, 62
and transfer of toxin
  from C. tetani cells, 41
treatment to interfere
  with toxin action, 73
virulence factor genet-
  ics, 75
protein trafficking, 78
proton pump, 76
psychological problems
  as effect of tetanus, 51
  tetanus toxin as treat-
    ment for, 80–81
puncture wounds
  and C. tetani growth, 38
  and oxygen deprivation, 12

rabbits
  immunization tests,
    26–27
  tetanus from soil particle
    injection, 23
  tetanus injection experi-
    ments, 22
  vaccine tests, 31
rabies, 17
Rajasinghe (king of
  Sithawatke, Sri Lanka),
  21
Ramon, Gaston, 31–35, 54
Rattone, Giorgio, 22
recovery, from tetanus, 48
recovery period, from tetanus, 47, 51
red blood cells, for C. tetani
  nutrition, 39
regulation, of toxin pro-
  duction, 41–43

Index

religious/philosophical objections to vaccination, 68
respiration, 16
retrograde transport, 46, 91
reuptake, of serotonin, 80–81
risks, of not taking vaccine, 59, 62
risus sardonicus, 10, 14, 21, 91
Roebling, John A., 22

St. Kilda, Scotland, 23
Scotland, 23
sensor proteins, 42–43, 91
sequencing, of *C. tetani* genome, 73–76
serotonin reuptake, 80–81
sheep, 18
sheep blood serum, 23–24
"sickness of eight days," 23
side effects, of vaccination, 58–60
sigma factor, 41, 42, 91
single-dose vaccination, 72–73
snakebite, tetanus and, 71
SNARE proteins, 78, 91
sodium pump, 76
soil, as source of bacteria, 24, 57
soldiers, tetanus incidence among, 36
spasms. *See* muscle spasms
spider bites, 17
spinal cord, transport of tetanus toxin to, 44–47
spine injury, 81–82
splinters, 14
spores
    and continued need for vaccinations, 57
    defined, 91
    longevity of, 11–12, 38
    and neonatal tetanus in Pakistan, 70

and spread of tetanus in St. Kilda, Scotland, 23
and survival of *C. tetani,* 15
transmission electron micrograph of, 39
stool samples, 11
Streptococcus gordonii, 73
stroke, 17
Strong, George Crockett, 22
strychnine, 24, 91
strychnine poisoning, 17
sucrose, 76
sulfur-sulfur bond, 44
survival rate, 49–50
symptoms
    confusion with other diseases, 17–18
    first appearance after infection. *See* incubation period
    treatment of, 50–51
synapse, 44–45, 47
synaptic vesicles, 45–46, 91
synaptobrevin, 47, 78, 91

tapioca, 33
Tay-Sachs disease, 81
Tenbroeck, C., 11
testing
    of isolated *C. tetani* bacterium, 26
    for tetanus, 17
    of vaccines, 19, 32
tetanolysin, 39, 75
tetanospasmin (tetanus toxin)
    action inside nerves, 47
    activation, 43–44
    as cause of tetanus symptoms, 40–41
    cross-linking, 56
    defined, 91
    genetic manipulation for production, 77
    inactivation, 73

isolation, 26
neutralization as part of treatment, 50
potency, 15
production by bacteria, 12
as protein delivery system, 81–83
for psychological disorder treatment, 80–81
regulation of production, 41–43
and repeat cases of tetanus, 62
transport to spinal cord, 44–47
treatment for action on nerves, 73
virulence factor, 41
tetanus (defined), 91
tetanus immunoglobulin
    for animal surgery, 28
    defined, 27, 91
    discovery of, 26–29
    and early forms of treatment, 52
    horses for production of, 29, 31–32, 50
    for treatment, 50, 51
    during World War I, 37
tetanus toxin. *See* tetanospasmin
tetanus toxoid, 49, 72–73
*tet*R gene, 41–43, 74, 75, 77
TetR protein, 41–42
*tet*X gene, 41, 42, 74
therapeutic usefulness, of toxins, 72
Thomson, Fred, 22
Thoreau, John, I, 22
tooth abscess, 17
toxin (defined), 92
toxin, tetanus. *See* tetanospasmin
toxoid, 32, 57, 92
tracheotomy, 50
traditional medicine, 70

transcription, 41–42, 75, 92

transport, of tetanus toxin to spinal cord, 44–47

transposon, 76, 92

treatment, 48–54

trismus, 14, 92

Tserclaes, Johann, 21

tsunami (2004), 68–69

Tychon, 20–21

umbilical cord, neonatal tetanus and, 16, 23, 55, 70

United Kingdom, 65

United States
  mortality rate (1900-2000), 69
  mortality rate (1940s), 10, 49, 69
  mortality rate (current), 50, 70
  recent status of tetanus in, 69–70
  tetanus incidence (1947-2004), 36

unvaccinated individuals, natural immunity in, 62–63

upstream activating sequence (UAS), 79, 92

urban environment, 10–11

vaccination
  deaths from, 18–19
  in developing countries, 70–71
  effect on U.S. mortality rate, 69–70
  fallacies about dangers of, 61–62
  multiple, 34
  and neonatal tetanus, 16, 55
  possible deaths from, 59
  religious/philosophical objections to, 68
  schedule for, 58
  single-dose, 72–73
  tetanus in vaccinated individuals, 65–66
  and tetanus treatment, 51

vaccine, 49. *See also* tetanus immunoglobulin
  adjuvants for, 61
  development of, 29–35, 37, 54
  and genetic engineering, 77
  manufacture of, 55–57
  safety of, 58–60
  side effects, 58

Vaccine Adverse Event Reporting System (VAERS), 59

Vallee, H., 30–31

VAMP (vesicle-associated membrane protein), 78

Vella, Luigi, 52

vesicles. *See* synaptic vesicles

veterinary medicine, 28

virulence factors, 41, 74–75, 92

Warbasse, J., 47

whooping cough, DPT shot for, 57

World Health Organization (WHO), 70, 72

World War I, 30–31, 36, 37

World War II, 35–37

wounds
  and *C. tetani* growth, 38
  and *C. tetani*'s entry into body, 12
  and tetanus treatment, 51
  types, leading to tetanus, 13

Zoller, C., 33, 54

About the Author

Patrick Guilfoile earned his Ph.D. in Bacteriology at the University of Wisconsin-Madison. He subsequently did postdoctoral research at the Whitehead Institute for Biomedical Research at the Massachusetts Institute of Technology. He is now a professor of biology at Bemidji State University in northern Minnesota, where he teaches microbiology and medical microbiology. His most recent research has focused on the molecular genetics of ticks and other parasites. He has authored or coauthored over 20 papers in scientific and biology education journals. He has also written a book in this series on antibiotic-resistant bacteria, a molecular biology laboratory manual, and a book on controlling ticks that transmit Lyme disease.

About the Consulting Editor

Hilary Babcock, M.D., M.P.H., is an Instructor in Medicine in the Infectious Diseases Division of Washington University School of Medicine and the Medical Director of Occupational Infection Control at Barnes-Jewish Hospital and St. Louis Children's Hospital. She is a graduate of Brown University and holds an M.D. from the University of Texas Southwestern Medical School, as well as an M.P.H. from St. Louis University. She has lectured, taught, and written extensively about infectious diseases, their treatment, and their prevention. She is a member of numerous medical associations and is board certified in infectious disease. She lives in St. Louis, Missouri.